Beginning
Classroom Guitar

Beginning
Classroom Guitar
with CD

A Musician's Approach

Second Edition

PHILIP HEMMO

SCHIRMER
CENGAGE Learning

Australia • Brazil • Japan • Korea • Mexico • Singapore • Spain • United Kingdom • United States

Beginning Classroom Guitar with CD:
A Musician's Approach, Second Edition
Philip Hemmo

Publisher, Music: Clark Baxter

Assistant Editor: Julie Yardley

Editorial Assistant: Eno Sarris

Technology Project Manager: Jennifer Ellis

Marketing Manager: Mark D. Orr

Marketing Assistant: Kristi Bostock

Advertising Project Manager: Brian Chaffee

Project Manager, Editorial Production:
Emily Smith

Print/Media Buyer: Kristine Waller

Permissions Editor: Kiely Sexton

Production Service:
Stratford Publishing Services

Copy Editor: Carrie Crompton

Illustrator: Highland Engraving

Compositor: Stratford Publishing Services

Cover Designer: Ark Stein

For product information and technology assistance, contact us at
Cengage Learning Customer & Sales Support, 1-800-354-9706

For permission to use material from this text or product, submit all requests online at **www.cengage.com/permissions**
Further permissions questions can be emailed to
permissionrequest@cengage.com

Library of Congress Control Number: 2003101141

ISBN-13: 978-0-534-17432-3
ISBN-10: 0-534-17432-9

Wadsworth
25 Thomson Place
Boston, MA 02210
USA

Cengage Learning is a leading provider of customized learning solutions with office locations around the globe, including Singapore, the United Kingdom, Australia, Mexico, Brazil and Japan. Locate your local office at: **international.cengage.com/region**

Cengage Learning products are represented in Canada by Nelson Education, Ltd.

For your course and learning solutions, visit **academic.cengage.com**
Purchase any of our products at your local college store or at our preferred online store **www.ichapters.com**

Printed in the United States of America
4 5 6 7 8 11 10 09 08

Contents

CD Program

A special thanks to all those who provided help or inspiration:
Tom Patterson, Douglas Rubio,
and my wife Dorothy who waited to try out every page.

About the Author

Classical guitarist Philip Hemmo has had the good fortune to study with many of the world's most influential players and pedagogues. He holds degrees in Classical Guitar Performance from the University of Arizona and Illinois State University. Mr. Hemmo has performed numerous concerts throughout the United States and Mexico. His teachers have included Thomas Patterson, Todd Seelye, and Douglas Rubio. Mr. Hemmo has participated in master classes/workshops with such performers as Sharon Isbin, William Kanengiser, David Russell, and Abel Carlevaro just to name a few. He has served on the faculty of the University of Arizona as well as in his current position directing the Guitar Studies program for Pima Community College where he specializes in classical guitar pedagogy and private instruction.

From the Author

Foreword

As a teacher, I know the importance of a good textbook to help teach new or foreign concepts. Over the years I have searched for a guitar text that allows a student not only to become a good guitar player but a good musician. This text was nowhere to be found. I hope you agree that what follows accomplishes both of my goals.

Please feel free to contact me at ph@southwestguitar.com

To the Beginning Guitar Student

Included in this textbook is all the information needed to help you learn to play the guitar. In designing this text I tried to choose pieces that I found fun and interesting while still providing the needed graded exercise. Practice each exercise, focusing on continuity and reading the music. Although at times it may be difficult, try not to memorize the music. This will help build up your music reading skills which, in turn, will allow you to play more difficult works with less difficulty. Follow all examples exactly. When working on new exercises, practice them slowly, concerning yourself with clear and even playing. Above all, *have fun* and enjoy the guitar.

To the Advanced Guitar Student

Use the information included in this textbook to refine the skills that you already have. Pay close attention to the musical examples. Build your music reading skills by not memorizing examples. The skills needed to expand your playing abilities are closely tied to your ability to read music. Follow all examples exactly. Numerous graded musical compositions are included to help you build your repertoire. In addition, follow the graded technical exercises to help refine your playing. When working on new exercises or compositions practice them slowly, concerning yourself with clear and even playing. Above all, *have fun* and enjoy the guitar.

Philip Hemmo

Part I
Getting Started

How to Read Music

Reading music is easy! Just think of the alphabet. The musical alphabet uses the letters A through G to notate pitches on a staff. Just think of the musical alphabet as a wheel. Moving clockwise from note to note takes us higher in pitch. Moving counterclockwise moves us lower in pitch. The musical alphabet repeats endlessly in either direction.

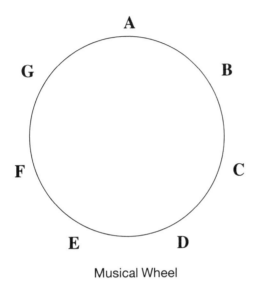

Musical Wheel

Now that we know what notes are in the musical alphabet, let's learn how we notate them. Notes are notated on the staff. The staff is made up of lines and spaces.

As you can see, the staff begins with a clef sign. All guitar music is in the treble clef. By having a reference note(s) on the staff, and using the musical wheel, you can identify any note anywhere. Luckily for us, the word F-A-C-E makes up the spaces of the staff.

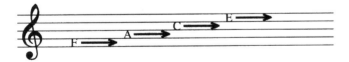

By using the musical wheel from any of these starting points we can find any note. Moving clockwise on the wheel is the same as moving upward on the staff. Likewise, moving counterclockwise is the same as moving lower on the staff.

Higher

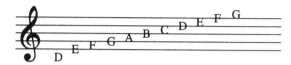

Lower

Rhythm

In music we use different types of notation to indicate the duration of a particular sound. We measure the length of these sounds by their number of pulses or beats.

    A *whole note* **o** is held for *four* beats/pulses.

o

1 – 2 – 3 – 4

    A *half note* ♩/♪ is held for *two* beats/pulses.

♩

1 – 2

    A *quarter note* ●/♪ is held for *one* beat/pulse.

♩

1

Bar Lines and Measures

Bar lines and the **measures** they create are used in music to make counting easier. Please note the double bar, which tells us we have reached the end of a piece.

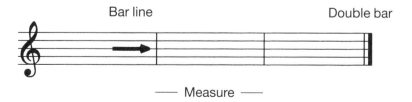

— Measure —

Time Signature

The **time signature** is a stack of two numbers at the beginning of a piece that tells what kind of note gets a beat and how many beats there are per measure. In the following example, each measure will have four beats with a quarter note equal to one beat.

# of beats/pulses per measure

What note value equals one beat?

How to Practice

What are the most effective ways to practice the guitar? This is an easy question with a straightforward answer. Effective practice for any level player consists of three elements: **Consistency**, **Continuity**, and **Planning**. I will discuss each concept and why it is important to your daily practice routine.

Consistency means being methodical in the way you practice. Keeping the same structure in your daily practice is the best way to achieve this. Have a set schedule for your daily practice sessions. (Example: 10 minutes for chords, 20 minutes for new songs, 10 minutes for old songs, etc.)

Continuity means practicing for a given amount of time each day. New concepts or ideas build on old ones. Think of a weight lifter who works out only on odd days. Compare him to the weight lifter who works out daily. The daily practice allows for more effective use of time to accomplish specific goals. This is true of most skills that require repetition.

Planning is the most important concept of the three. It allows us to define specific goals in our daily practice and to see their evolution over larger periods of time. (Example: I need to know page 22 for next week's test.) By planning what goals will be achieved in a specific time frame, we can fully utilize the practice time at hand.

Try to consider these three concepts when designing your daily practice routine. The recommended practice time for students using this textbook is from 30 to 45 minutes daily. Some students may find it useful to use a daily log to chart progress.

Parts of the Guitar

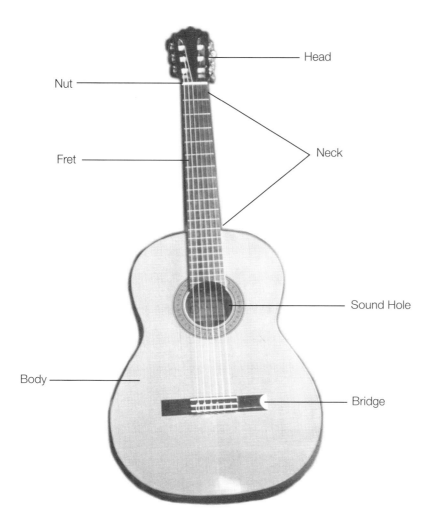

Head

Nut

Fret

Neck

Sound Hole

Body

Bridge

Sitting Position

Let's talk about a good sitting position. This is a very important part of learning to play the guitar. We want to facilitate ease of motion and relaxation, which will in turn make playing easier and more fun. The sitting position I recommend is the so-called "classical" sitting position. I will show that this position is the most beneficial whatever style of music you intend to play.

The image that immediately comes to mind when you think of someone playing the guitar is a standing performer with his/her guitar supported by a strap. If we take this position (without the strap) and sit down we have the basics of the "classical" sitting position.

Standing with the guitar.

The "classical" sitting position.

When sitting with the guitar, sit on the front third of your chair. Keep your back straight while sitting squarely on the chair. Your guitar should be touching your body at three points: your mid-chest, your left thigh, and the top of your right thigh. Tilt the guitar at a slight angle away from your body. In addition, the head of your guitar should be at about eye level. Use something sturdy to support your left leg (a guitar case works well). This will help simulate a standing guitar position while seated.

The goal of this sitting position is to provide a feeling of balance as well as one of relaxation. Consciously think about your sitting position when you start to practice. This may seem a little awkward at first, but it is important to make playing as comfortable and easy as possible.

The Hands

We have specific terminology to indicate the fingers of the left and right hands:

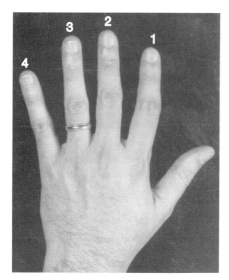

Left Hand

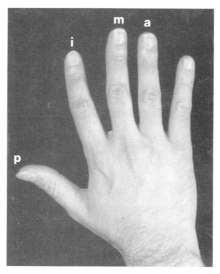

Right Hand

The right hand fingers are notated by letters that come from the Spanish words for each finger:

p	*pulgar*	thumb
i	*indice*	index finger
m	*medico*	middle finger
a	*anular*	ring finger

The left hand fingers are represented by numbers rather than letters. This system is consistent in all modern guitar music.

1	index finger
2	middle finger
3	ring finger
4	pinky

Nail Shape and Care

The shape and care of your nails will become more important as we begin to play more difficult music. I suggest you start to grow your nails out now so they are a good length when you need them.

Since each individual's hands are unique, there are no set rules for nail shape. With this in mind I have found that the best results come about when you consider the string's point of view. Remember, our end goal is to be able to use our nail to displace the string with a minimal amount of effort and produce a loud, clear sound. To achieve this I suggest a slightly off-centered peak on fingers i, m, and a. This provides the most displacement of the string with the least amount of energy.

The concept for your thumb is similar. Again, we want the best sound with the least amount of effort. To achieve this I suggest a bit more playing surface. This also allows for more control of the sound.

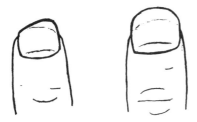

Shape for i, m, and a.   Shape for p.

Keeping your nails in good condition will take a little work every day. There are two basic steps for daily nail care: **Filing** and **Finishing**.

Filing is very important. It allows you to refine the shape of your nails and keep them at the desired length. I recommend a sapphire or diamond dust nail file. This type of file evenly files the nail surface. Although the rate at which your nails grow will vary, you should plan on filing them on a fairly regular basis.

Finishing refines the nail surface. After you have shaped your nails the surface is left rough. In order to smooth out the surface a fine emery board or sandpaper will be needed. These are sold by grade. A 500–600 grade board or paper is best. You should polish your nails after shaping, before playing, after long practice sessions, or as needed.

Right/Left Hand Positions

Right Hand Position

The ideal right hand position allows for both relaxation and freedom of movement. To achieve this follow these steps:

1. Shake out your right hand. This will allow you to completely relax your hand.

2. Place your arm over the guitar, resting your upper forearm on the guitar.

3. Add a slight arch to your wrist. This will allow for easy movement of both your fingers and thumb.

4. Get ready to play.

Right Hand Position

Left Hand Position

The best left hand position allows strength and relaxation at the same time. To achieve this, several things must be remembered:

1. The left hand thumb should be placed in the middle of the back of the neck. Use the ball of your thumb as a balance point.
2. Your fingers should be in a relaxed position parallel to the frets.
3. Drop your wrist so that your palm does not touch the bottom of the neck.
4. Allow your elbow to control all large movements.

Left Hand Position

Rest Strokes and Free Strokes

Rest strokes and **free strokes** are two different right hand techniques that you will use when practicing. Throughout this textbook rest strokes should be practiced on single line melodies. Free strokes will be used when we begin our study of arpeggios.

Rest Strokes

To play rest strokes, begin from a relaxed right hand position. Put your i finger on the first string. The concept of preparing to play a note is called **preparation**. From this point provide enough energy for your finger to push through the first string. Your goal is to follow through and land your finger on the second string. At this point prepare your m finger on the first string and repeat the process. As each finger plays, the other relaxes and prepares to play again. This process is called **alternating i-m rest strokes**. Use alternating i-m rest strokes for all single line exercises within this textbook.

Preparing to play a rest stroke.

Follow through.

Free Strokes

Free strokes are strokes that do not follow through and land on the next string. The direction of these strokes is back into the hand. To play a free stroke, prepare i on the third string. Move through the string, aiming for your palm. The stroke itself has a motion very similar to scratching.

Preparing to play a free stroke.

Follow through.

Using a Guitar Pick (Plectrum)

Using a guitar pick is easy. Pinch the pick between your thumb and first finger. Allow about ⅓ to ¼ of the pick to stick out. Play using motion from your wrist.

Holding a pick.

Tuning Your Guitar

Tuning your guitar is a skill you should begin to practice right away. It is not difficult to tune your guitar, but it may take a little time to train your ear. Try not to get frustrated. Think of it as a game. Here is your winning game plan:

1. We will start by tuning the low (6) string of the guitar. This should be done by matching pitch with an E tuning fork, a pitch pipe, or a piano. On the piano play the white key immediately to the right of the group of two black keys. This note is E. After you hear the note from the piano, tuning fork, or pitch pipe, try to remember the sound. The best way to do this is to hum the note. Play the open sixth string. Establish which is higher in pitch: the note you are humming or the note you played on the guitar. Then proceed to turn the tuning machine for the sixth string. Continue in the same direction until both notes sound the same. Do not change directions unless you are positive that you have gone too far.

2. Once the sixth string is in tune the rest is fairly easy. To tune the fifth string, play the sixth string at the fifth fret. This pitch should be the same as the open fifth string. As before, continue in the same direction (tightening/loosening) until either the notes match or you are sure that you are way off.

3. To tune the fourth string, play the fifth string at the fifth fret. This pitch will be the same as the open fourth string.

4. To tune the third string, play the fourth string at the fifth fret. This will equal the open third string.

5. To tune the second string, play the third string at the fourth fret. This will equal the open second string.

6. To tune the first string, play the second string at the fifth fret. This will equal the open first (high) string.

Low 6th String   High 1st String

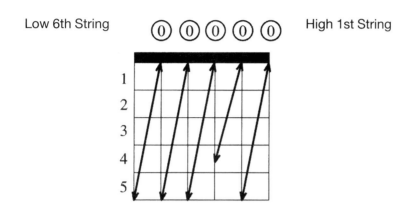

As I said, tuning your guitar will take practice. Try to tune your guitar every day. If you do not have access to a piano, tuning fork, or pitch pipe, practice tuning your guitar to whatever pitch the sixth string is currently tuned.

Part II
Reading Music

Open String Notes

The six strings on the guitar are notated using the numbers one through six. The string numbered one is the highest pitched string. From your perspective it is the farthest away. Here is an easy way to remember all six of the open strings. The bold letter indicates the note name for each open string.

(1) (high) **E**aster

(2)   **B**unny

(3)   **G**ets

(4)   **D**epressed

(5)   **A**fter

(6) (low) **E**aster

Open String Rest Strokes

We use rest strokes to bring out single line melodies. As we learn to read music this technique will help us to build accuracy. Practice alternating i-m rest strokes on the first string. Try to keep the rhythm steady and even. This exercise will help you to feel comfortable playing rest strokes. Keep these ideas in mind:

1. Play loud! This will help build confidence.

2. After each finger plays, allow it to relax, thus preparing it to play again.

3. Make sure each finger stroke goes through the first string, landing on the next string.

When you feel comfortable with playing on the first string, use the same procedure on the second string.

And now for some music!

Notes on the First (E) String

There are three notes to learn on the first string of the guitar. These notes are E, F, & G.

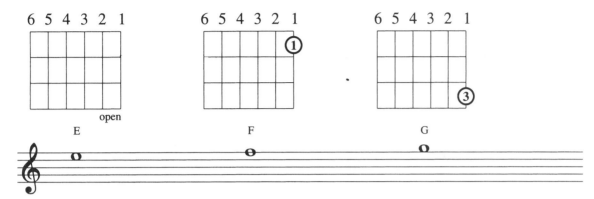

To play E, simply strike the open first string. To play F, use your first finger to push down the first string just before the first fret. To play G, use your third finger to push down the first string just before the third fret.

First string exercises

Following are three easy exercises that use the notes on the first string:

Remember to practice these slowly, reading the music. At first do not be concerned with speed, just accuracy. Use both rest strokes and a pick for these exercises.

Chord Break #1

A chord occurs anytime you play two or more notes simultaneously. When you play a series of chords it is called a **chord progression**. Following, we will learn two chords, e minor and G.

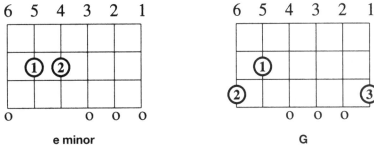

e minor   G

The O's indicate open strings.

To play e minor, put your first finger on the fifth string on the second fret and your second finger on the fourth string on the second fret. Strum all six strings.

To play G, place your first finger on the fifth string on the second fret, your second finger on the sixth string on the third fret, and your third finger on the first string on the third fret. Using your pick/plectrum, strum all six strings.

Chord Progressions

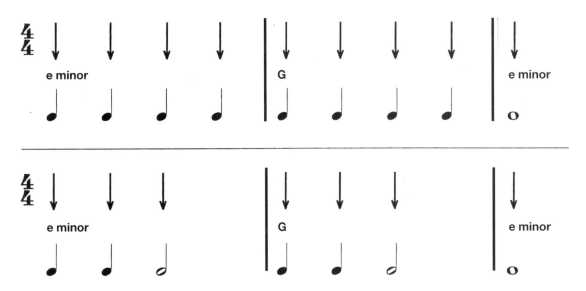

When switching between e minor and G remember that your first finger stays in the same place. This is what we call a **common finger**. Use the rhythms given. Practice playing slowly and evenly.

This chord progression is *very* similar to the progressions you will find in popular music. Groups like Nirvana, the Lemonheads, and many others use variations on these strumming patterns in their songs.

Notes on the Second (B) String

There are three notes to learn on the second string of the guitar. These notes are B, C, & D.

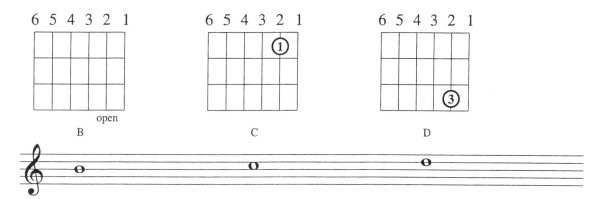

To play B, simply strike the open second string. To play C, use your first finger to push down the second string just before the first fret. To play D, use your third finger to push down the second string just before the third fret.

Second string exercises

Following are three easy exercises that use the notes on the first and second strings:

Remember to practice these slowly, reading the music. At first do not be concerned with speed, just accuracy. Use both rest strokes and a pick for these exercises.

First and Second String Exercises

The following exercises use the notes we have learned on the first two strings. Practice these exercises using both a pick and rest strokes.

CD Track 7   Tune #1   PH

CD Track 8   **Sleep, Sleep, Baby Sleep**
                              French Lullaby

CD Track 9   Ode to Joy   Beethoven

CD Track 10   **Lightly Row**

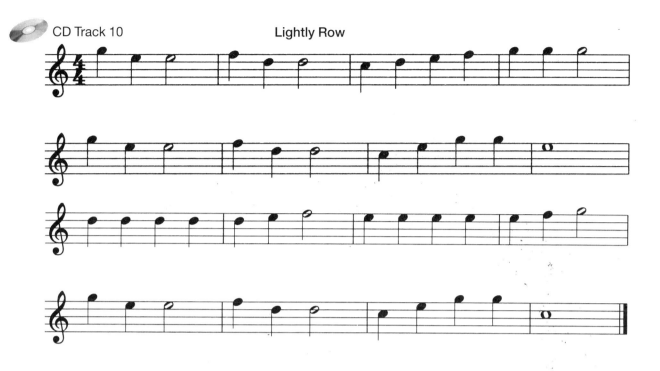

It is important to start to develop the skills needed to play with other musicians. The following duet will help in this endeavor. The most difficult aspect of ensemble playing is timing. Practice tapping your foot to keep the beat.

Guitar 1   **Duet**   PH

Guitar 2

Guitar 1

Guitar 2

Chord Break #2

Let's expand our chord vocabulary by learning two new chords: C and G7.

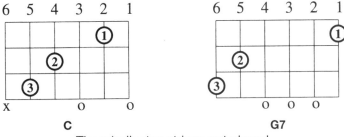

The x indicates strings not played.

To play C, put your first finger on the second string on the first fret, your second finger on the fourth string on the second fret, and your third finger on the fifth string on the third fret. Strum strings five-four-three-two-one.

To play G7, place your first finger on the first string on the first fret, your second finger on the fifth string on the second fret, and your third finger on the sixth string on the third fret. Strum all six strings.

Chord Progressions

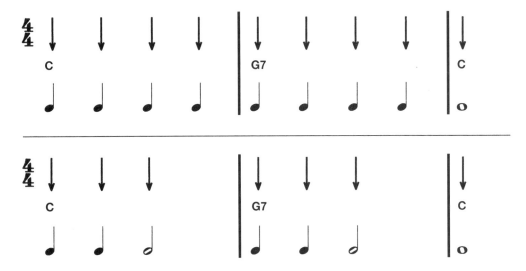

When switching between C and G7 notice that the overall shape remains similar. Use the rhythms given. Practice playing slowly and evenly.

The following progression is very common in country/western music. In this example the lowest note of the chord or **bass** is plucked followed by two strums of the chord. The number within the circle tells us which string to pluck. The rhythm of this example feels like a waltz.

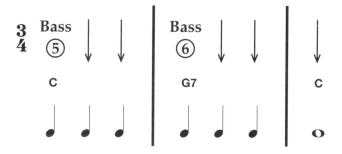

Notes on the Third (G) String

There are only two notes to learn on the third string of the guitar. These notes are G & A.

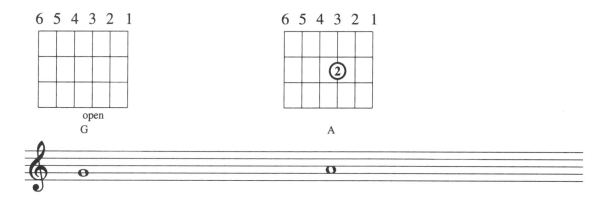

To play G, strike the open third string. To play A, use your second finger to push down the third string just before the second fret.

Third string exercises

Following are three easy exercises that use the notes on the first three strings:

In the third exercise, we play from the G on the third string to the G on the first string. This distance is called an **octave**. An octave is the distance between two notes with the same letter name that are higher or lower than one another.

As before, remember to practice these slowly, reading the music. At first do not be concerned with speed, just accuracy. Use both rest strokes and a pick for these exercises.

Exercises on the First Three Strings

The following exercises use the notes we have learned on the first three strings. Practice these exercises using both a pick and rest strokes.

CD Track 11   **Bye, Baby Bunting**
                                        English Lullaby

CD Track 12   **Yankee Doodle**

CD Track 13   **Red River Valley**

Here are two more exercises on the first three strings to practice. Notice the double bar with the two dots. This is a repeat sign. This tells us to repeat all the prior material.

CD Track 14

Clair de Lune
French Folksong

Repeat Sign

CD Track 15

Half note rest: 2 beats of silence

Simple Gifts

Here are two more exercises on the first three strings to practice.

CD Track 16   **Aura Lee**

CD Track 17   **Don't You Weep After Me**

Chord Break #3

Let's expand our chord vocabulary by adding two more chords: D and A7.

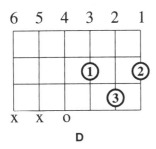 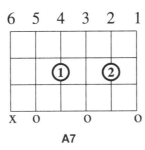

To play D, simply put your first finger on the third string on the second fret, your second finger on the first string on the second fret, and your third finger on the second string on the third fret. Strum strings four-three-two-one.

To play A7, place your first finger on the fourth string on the second fret and your second finger on the second string on the second fret. Strum strings five-four-three-two-one.

Chord Progressions

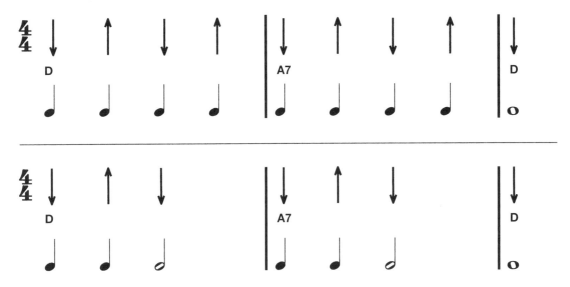

When switching between D and A7, remember that the overall shape will remain the same. This is what we call a **common shape**. Use the rhythms given. Practice playing slowly and evenly, using both down and up strokes.

Now that we have mastered e minor, G, C, G7, D, and A7, try the following more challenging chord progressions.

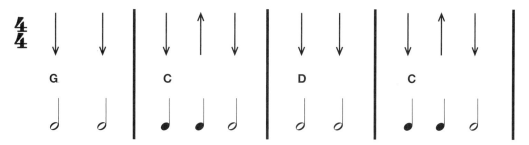

These progressions are very common in popular music. Listen for them in songs by Weezer, the Kingsmen, and the Beatles.

Notes on the Fourth (D) String

There are three notes to learn on the fourth string of the guitar. These notes are D, E, & F.

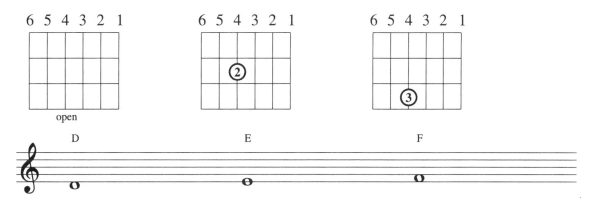

To play D, simply strike the open fourth string. To play E, use your second finger to push down the fourth string just before the second fret. To play F, use your third finger to push down the fourth string just before the third fret.

Fourth string exercises

Following are two easy exercises that use the notes on the first four strings:

As before, remember to practice these slowly, reading the music. At first do not be concerned with speed, just accuracy. Use both rest strokes and a pick for these exercises.

Exercises on the First Four Strings

The following exercises use the notes we have learned on the first four strings. Practice these exercises using both a pick and rest strokes.

The first two exercises use a new time signature, 3/4. This indicates that there are three beats per measure. The quarter note still equals one beat/pulse. The following exercise also has a new rhythmic value, the dotted half note. A dot increases a note's duration by half the original amount. In this case, the dot adds one beat to the value of the half note, for a total of three beats.

Each of the following pieces begins with an incomplete measure called a pick-up. The pick-up helps lead us into the piece.

CD Track 18   **Amazing Grace**

CD Track 19   **Spanish Ladies**

I Gave My Love a Cherry

The following duet uses notes on all four strings. As in the previous duet, practice tapping your foot to keep time.

Duet   PH

A **tie**  rhythmically connects two notes of the same pitch across a bar line. Instead of replaying the second note, just sustain the first note for the duration of both.

1 - 2 - 3 - 4 - 1 - 2 - 3 - 4

Now try the following piece that uses ties.

CD Track 21   **When the Saints Go Marching In**

The next piece is a round. A round is a type of piece where two or more voices (or guitars) play the same music but start at different times. In the following three-part round the first player will begin the piece. When guitar one reaches the star in the score the second player will begin. When guitar two reaches the star, the third player will begin. The piece may be played through as many times as the players wish. Each player will stop at the double bar.

Three-Part Round

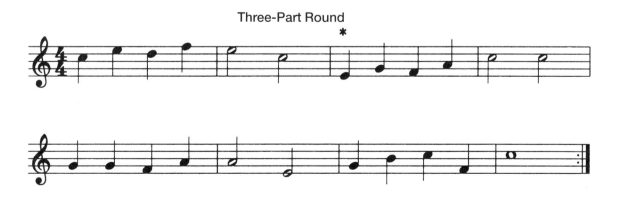

Chord Break #4

Let's expand our chord vocabulary by adding two more chords: D Sus, A, and review D.

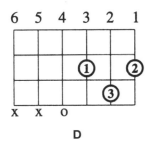

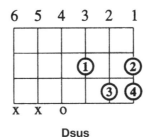

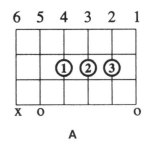

To play D Sus, put your first finger on the third string on the second fret, your third finger on the second string on the third fret, and your fourth finger on the first string on the third fret. Strum strings four-three-two-one.

To play A, place your first finger on the fourth string on the second fret and your second finger on the third string on the second fret, and your third finger on the second string on the second fret. Strum strings five-four-three-two-one.

We already know how to play the D chord.

Chord Progression:

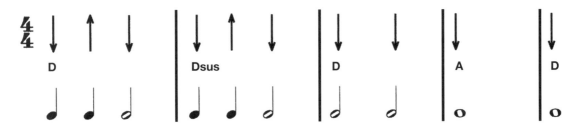

Of all the chord progressions we have worked on so far this is by far the most difficult. I suggest you practice each individual chord change before attempting the overall progression. Try to remember what type of movement each finger will make. This will help to eliminate confusion.

You can find variations of this progression in songs by Queen, Rush, Tom Petty & the Heartbreakers, and many more popular artists.

Notes on the Fifth (A) String

There are three notes to learn on the fifth string of the guitar. These notes are A, B, & C.

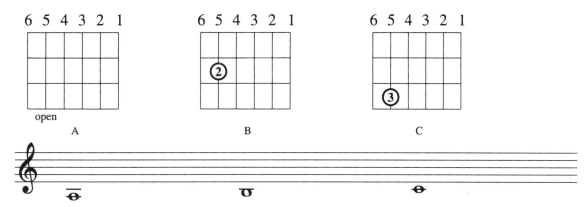

To play A, strike the open fifth string. To play B, use your second finger to push down the fifth string just before the second fret. To play C, use your third finger to push down the fifth string just before the third fret.

Fifth string exercises

Following are two easy exercises that use the notes on the first five strings:

The third exercise uses **eighth notes** ♪. Eighth notes equal a half beat. Two eighth notes are equivalent to a quarter note.

CD Track 22   Eighth notes beamed together.

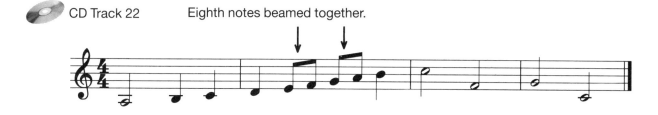

Exercises on the First Five Strings

The following exercises use the notes we have learned on the first five strings. Practice these exercises using both a pick and rest strokes. The dotted quarter notes ♩. are worth one and a half beats.

To help keep track of the half beats, subdivide your counting by adding '&' in between numbered beats.

1 & 2 & 3 & 4 &   1 & 2 &   3 & 4 &   1 & 2 & 3 & 4 &   1 & 2 & 3 & 4 &

CD Track 23   Greensleeves

CD Track 24   **My Country 'Tis of Thee**   Henry Carey

Sometimes it is necessary to repeat only part of a piece. The following piece is an example of ternary (three part) form. The *D. C. al Fine* stands for *Da Capo al Fine*: from the beginning to the end. This direction tells us that once we have played through the entire piece we should go back to the beginning and proceed until the *Fine* (end).

CD Track 25   **L'Homme Armé**
                    French Renaissance melody

Duet   PH

The following exercises include another new rhythm, the triplet. The triplet is another subdivision of the beat. As we have learned, two eighth notes equal one quarter note. The triplet subdivides the quarter note into three parts.

   To help count triplets, subdivide your counting by saying tri-pi-let for each group of three eighth note triplets in the following exercise.

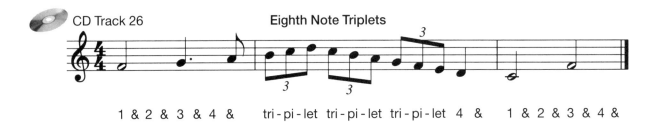

CD Track 26   **Eighth Note Triplets**

1 & 2 & 3 & 4 &   tri - pi - let tri - pi - let tri - pi - let 4 &   1 & 2 & 3 & 4 &

Now try this famous lullaby by Johannes Brahms (1833–1897). Be aware of the triplet in the last line (*).

CD Track 27   **Lullaby**   J. Brahms

When practicing these new exercises, remember to keep the quarter note pulse even. By keeping a steady quarter note pulse you will be able to count the subdivisions within each beat. You may wish to clap or vocalize each exercise before beginning to play it on the guitar. Don't be frustrated if you don't get them right away. Try adjusting your tempo to a slow enough tempo so you can control the beat.

Guitar Ensemble

The following exercises are for three or four guitars. Perform them in the same way that you did the previous round.

CD Track 28   **Are You Sleeping**

The double bar at the end of this piece instructs you to repeat the piece from the beginning.

CD Track 29 Round C. Bresgen

CD Track 30 Round PH

Practice these pieces slowly while carefully tapping a steady rhythm. This is the key to effective ensemble playing. In addition, guitar 1 should count out a preliminary measure of pulses at the desired tempo.

Chord Break #5

Let's expand our chord vocabulary by adding another new chord: E. The following chord progressions will also use A and G.

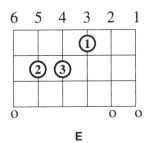

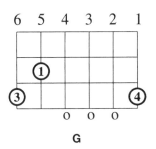

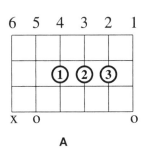

To play E, simply put your first finger on the third string on the first fret, your second finger on the fifth string on the second fret, and your third finger on the fourth string on the second fret. Strum strings six-five-four-three-two-one.

We already know how to play both the G and A chords.

Chord Progressions

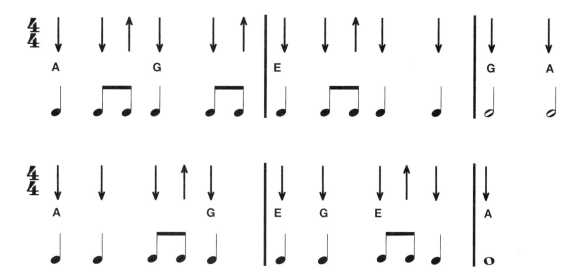

Notes on the Sixth (E) String

There are three notes to learn on the sixth string of the guitar. These notes are E, F, & G. If this looks familiar, it is. These are the same notes we learned on the first string, only two octaves lower.

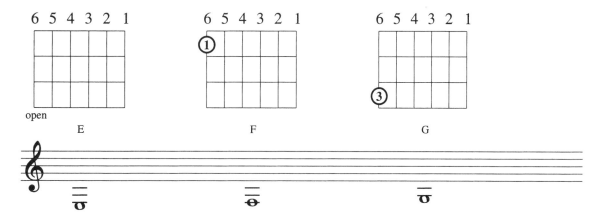

To play E, simply pluck the open first string. To play F, use your first finger to push down the first string just before the first fret. To play G, use your third finger to push down the first string just before the third fret.

Sixth string exercises

Following are two easy exercises that use the notes on all six strings:

As with all of the exercises we have learned, practice these slowly, reading the music. At first do not be concerned with speed, just accuracy. Use both rest strokes and a pick for these exercises.

Exercises on All Six Strings

The following exercises use the notes we have learned on all six strings. Practice these exercises using both a pick and rest strokes.

CD Track 31   Shenandoah

CD Track 32   **The Minstrel Boy**

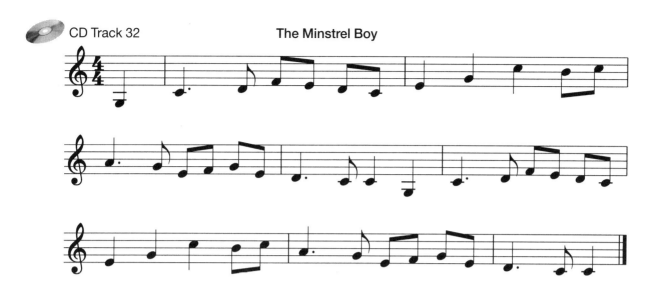

CD Track 33   **Fantasy in a Minor**

CD Track 34

Swing Low, Sweet Chariot

Fine

D.C. al Fine

Come Again! Sweet Love Doth Now Invite

John Dowland
(1563–1626)

Quarter note rest

Eighth note rest

When practicing "Come Again! Sweet Love . . . ," be aware of the quarter and eighth note rests.

CD Track 35

Blue-Tail Fly

Civil War tune

More Guitar Ensemble

The following exercises are for three or four guitars. Perform them in the
same way that you did the previous rounds.

Dona Nobis Pacem

CD Track 36

Oh, How Lovely Is the Evening

Chord Break #6

Let's expand our chord vocabulary by adding two new chords: a minor and d minor. We already know the C chord.

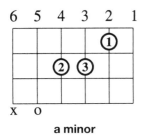

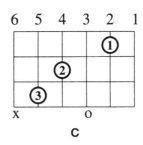

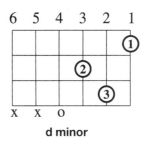

To play a minor, put your first finger on the second string on the first fret, your second finger on the fourth string on the second fret, and your third finger on the third string on the second fret. Strum strings five-four-three-two-one.

To play d minor, put your first finger on the first string on the first fret, your second finger on the third string on the second fret, and your third finger on the second string on the third fret. Strum strings four-three-two-one.

Chord Progression

The following chord progression consists of an alternating bass note and strum pattern. Use P (thumb) for the bass note, which will be on either the fourth or fifth string, and i, m, and a, for the top three notes of each chord on the first three strings. Use the bass note to help facilitate the chord change. Watch your right hand position. Use free strokes when playing i, m, and a.

 CD Track 37

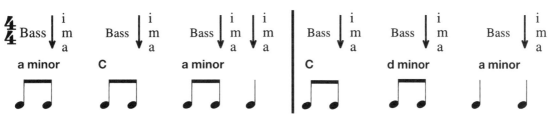

When switching between a minor and C, remember that there are two common fingers. The change from C to d minor is more difficult. Practice this progression with emphasis on playing slowly but changing quickly.

Waltz

We are now ready to learn our first piece of classical guitar music. The following piece is an excerpt from a waltz composed by Matteo Carcassi (1792–1853). A waltz is a type of dance characterized by a strong pulse followed by two weaker ones. This excerpt will require you to practice right hand free strokes as well as plucking two notes simultaneously. There are exercises in the technique anthology that will help make this easier.

All notes with down stems should be plucked with the thumb. All other notes will be plucked with alternating i and m free strokes. Right and left hand fingerings are given. Please follow them closely.

CD Track 38   **Waltz (excerpt)**   Matteo Carcassi
(1792–1853)

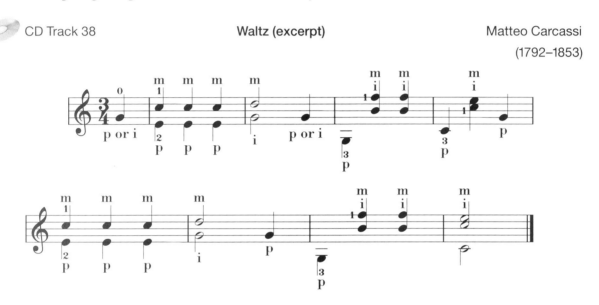

Practice this piece slowly until it feels comfortable. We have learned all of the notes used in this piece. The only thing new is how they are combined to create this work. This is much like the pieces you will hear on classical guitar recordings.

Compound Meter

All of the music we have studied to this point has been in simple meter. In simple meter the first beat of each measure usually receives a slight accent.

CD Track 39

1   2   3   4   1   2   3   4

In **compound meter** the basic beat is the dotted quarter note. The time signatures will usually have an eighth note as the lower number. To keep a steady pulse, count eighth notes. However, keep in mind that the accent patterns are in groupings of three.

CD Track 40

1 2 3 4   5   6   1 2 3 4 5 6

Pieces in compound meter have a much different rhythmic feeling than those in simple meter.

CD Track 41   Row, Row Your Boat

The following exercises use the notes we have learned on all six strings. The exercises are all in compound meter. Remember to count the eighth notes in groupings of three. Practice these exercises using both a pick and rest strokes.

CD Track 42   The Darby Ram

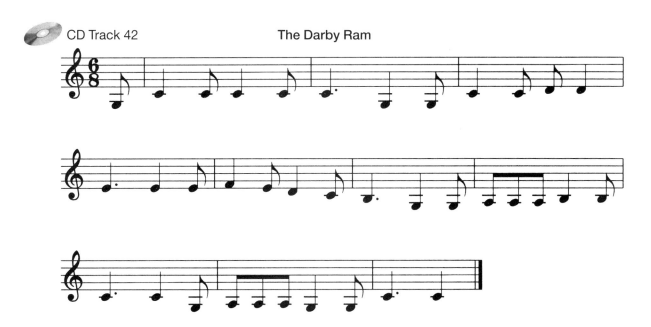

CD Track 43   **Drink to Me Only with Thine Eyes**

CD Track 44   **High Barbaree**

Song   Franz Schubert
                                          (1797–1828)

Chord Break #7

Let's expand our chord vocabulary by adding two new chords: E7 and B7.
The following chord progressions will also use A (with a new fingering)
and E.

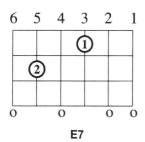

E7

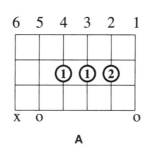

A

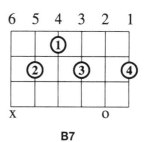

B7

To play E7, place your first finger on the third string on the first fret and
your second finger on the fifth string on the second fret. Strum strings six-
five-four-three-two-one.

To play B7, place your first finger on the fourth string on the first fret, your second finger on the fifth string on the second fret, your third finger on the third string on the second fret, and your fourth finger on the first string on the second fret. Strum strings five-four-three-two-one.

We already know how to play the A chord, but try this new fingering.

Chord Progressions

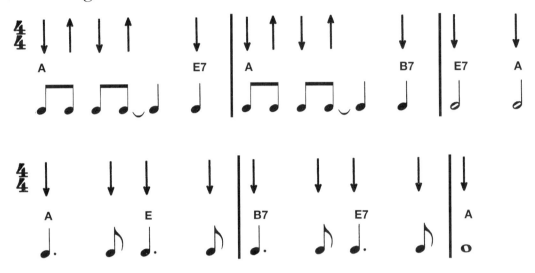

Guitar Tablature

If you plan to play any contemporary music (pop, rock, jazz, blues, etc.) you will undoubtably encounter **guitar tablature**. This system of notation has become very popular in the last several years. It is an easy shortcut when learning popular music.

The system of tablature used today for guitar music can be traced back to at least the early 1500s. Our earliest publications for lute, a relative of the guitar, are notated in tablature. The use of tablature allowed amateur musicians to learn music quickly and in volume. The system has persisted with few changes until today.

Guitar tablature utilizes a series of vertical lines, which represent each string of the guitar. The strings are ordered from high (the first string) to low (the sixth string).

High 1st String

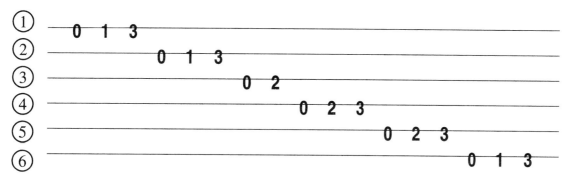

Low 6th String

Numbers are placed on the strings to indicate the fret to be played. You read the tablature from left to right just like music. Here are the notes we have learned so far in tablature.

Tablature is a quick and efficient way to learn popular music. The main limitation of our modern system is the lack of rhythmic notation. For this reason it is important to use traditional notation in conjunction with tablature to assure rhythmic precision.

Dynamics

In music we have a system to designate the volume of one event compared to another. We call this distinction **dynamics**. How do we know how loud or soft a particular note or chord should be? We use abbreviations for the Italian terms that describe degrees of volume.

Italian term	Abbreviation	Volume
pianissimo	*pp*	very soft
piano	*p*	soft
mezzo piano	*mp*	medium soft
mezzo forte	*mf*	medium loud
forte	*f*	loud
fortissimo	*ff*	very loud

I find it easy to think of dynamics in terms of a volume knob like the one on your stereo.

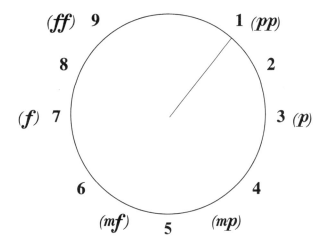

Within a piece we use two symbols to direct us to grow louder (*crescendo*) or softer (*decrescendo*).

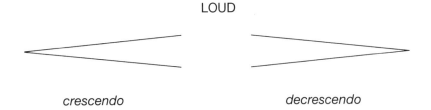

crescendo   decrescendo

Notes Everywhere on the Guitar

Now that we know all the natural notes in the open position (first three frets) of the guitar, let's learn how to find any note anywhere on the guitar. To do this we must learn about sharps ♯ and flats ♭. A **sharp** is a note that is one fret higher than its natural note. A **flat** is a note that is one fret lower than its natural note. If we apply sharps and flats to our musical wheel, it will look like this:

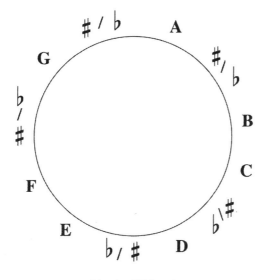

Musical Wheel

As you can see, some notes do not have a sharp or a flat. E and B have no sharp. C and F have no flat. This is because there is not a fret between these notes.

The next term we need to learn is **enharmonic**. We define enharmonic as a single sound/pitch that can be notated two different ways. That is why there is only one fret between notes with sharps/flats. This means that F sharp and G flat sound exactly the same and are played exactly the same way. You cannot tell the difference between these notes except by how they are notated on a staff.

By using the musical wheel you can now find any note anywhere on the guitar. Practice by beginning with an open string and moving higher fret by fret, naming each note as you go. When you reach the twelfth fret, you will have played an octave on one string. All of the strings reach an octave at the twelfth fret.

Sharps and Flats in Music

When reading music, you will encounter sharps and flats in one of two ways: either in a **key signature** or as **accidentals**.

Key Signature

A **key signature** occurs at the beginning of each line of music and tells us which notes in a piece are to be played sharp/flat. The sharp/flat notes apply to all notes with the same letter name no matter at which octave they are played.

The following example has two sharps in the key signature. All F and C notes will be played a half step higher as F# and C#. Remember, this applies to all F and C notes everywhere.

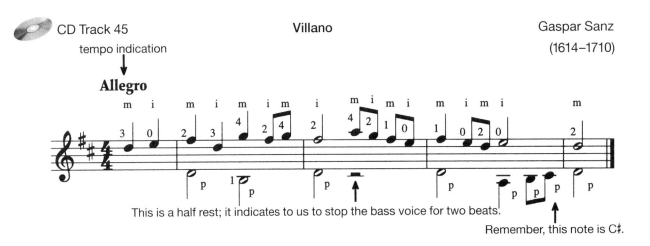

This is a half rest; it indicates to us to stop the bass voice for two beats.

Remember, this note is C#.

The preceding work is a lively Baroque dance that was composed for a relative of the modern guitar. We know it is intended to be played lively by the tempo indication at the beginning of the piece. A **tempo indication** tells us at what speed a work should be ideally performed. The tempo indicated is marked *Allegro* (fast moving, cheerful, or merry). Here is a list of the most common tempo indications and a definition.

Largo	slow or solemn
Larghetto	slowly with motion
Adagio	slowly and gently
Andante	a walking tempo
Moderato	a moderate tempo
Presto	quickly

Accidentals

The second possibility that you will encounter while reading music is when sharps/flats are used as accidentals. An **accidental** occurs when a sharp/flat is placed within a composition rather than in the key signature. The accidental applies only to the specific note it alters and is negated by the bar line at the end of the measure it is used in, or by a natural sign ♮.

The following piece uses an accidental in measure five. Remember, this applies only to like notes that occur after the accidental within the specific measure, and is negated by the bar line.

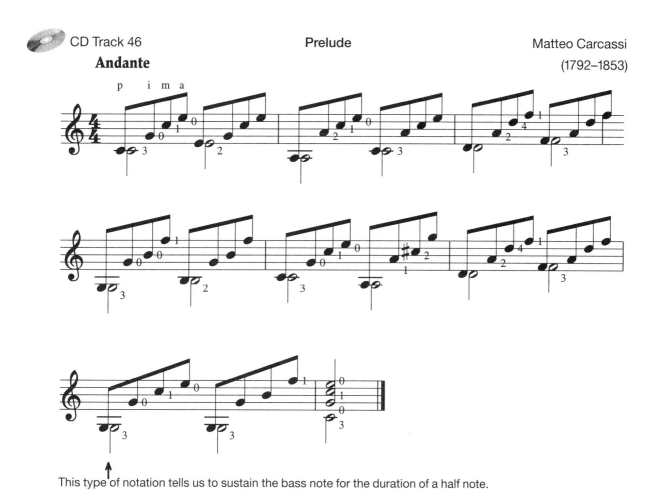

CD Track 46   Prelude   Matteo Carcassi
Andante   (1792–1853)

This type of notation tells us to sustain the bass note for the duration of a half note.

This prelude is an arpeggio study. Use the p-i-m-a arpeggio throughout. This study uses chords that we already know. The only difference is how we are using these chords.

These pieces should be practiced at a slow tempo with emphasis on even chord changes. In addition, when playing chords, do not be concerned with cutting off notes that occur within a particular chord. Use free strokes for both of the above works.

The above works are exactly like the types of pieces you will hear performed in classical guitar recitals.

Chord Break #8 (Basic Blues)

The basic blues pattern is a standard accompaniment pattern in many popular songs. To play this pattern we need to learn three new chords. We will also need different fingerings for A, D, and E.

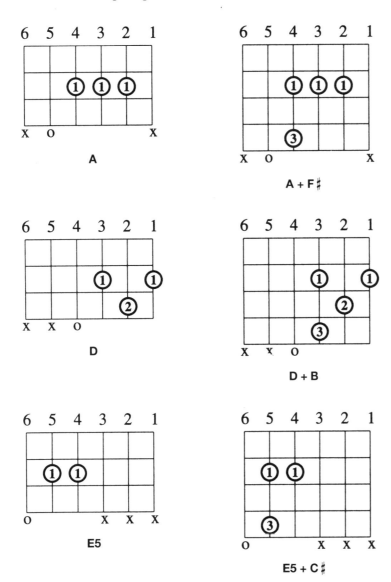

Observe all fingerings for the above chords. Especially important are the strings not played in each chord. These are notated with an **X**. The fingerings given require a single finger to cover more than one string. To do this, lay your finger flat on the indicated strings at the fret shown.

The following chord progression is a basic blues pattern in A. Remember to repeat each measure the indicated number of times.

Bar Chords

The next step in expanding our chord vocabulary involves learning about bar chords. If you listen to popular music you will be hard pressed to find a song that does not use bar chords. Most of the songs you hear on the radio use bar chords.

What is a bar chord?

A **bar chord** is a moveable chord in which the first finger replaces the open strings. Here is an example:

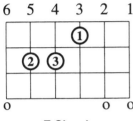

E Chord

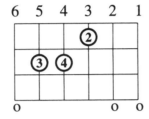

E Chord with alternate fingering

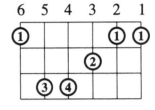

E-form bar chord

To play the E-form bar chord start by playing an E chord. Replace fingers 1, 2, and 3 with 2, 3, and 4. Move fingers 2, 3, and 4 forward 1 fret each. Place your first finger flat over the six strings at the first fret. The bar now imitates the open stringed notes of the open E chord.

This chord is moveable. This means that whatever note is on the sixth string, under the first finger, is the root of the chord. The above bar chord at the first fret is F.

Tips for easier bar chords

- Use your left hand thumb in opposition to your first finger. This will allow for the most efficient use of pressure to keep the bar down.

- When placing the bar, make sure you are right before the fret. You might also slightly roll your first finger toward the nut. This allows for the most efficient use of pressure.

- Try to only push down on the strings to be played. For example, for the E-form bar chord, push down on strings 6, 2, and 1. The other strings are fretted by other fingers.

Bar chords are tricky at first. Don't be frustrated if they don't sound correct right away. A little practice will help to build up strength in your first finger and flexibility in your bar.

There are two types of bar chords that are common to popular music; the E-form and the A-form bar chords.

E-form bar chords

The **E-form bar chord** is based around the open position shape of an E chord. This is true of all E-form bar chords. We have moveable chords based on the shape of E, E minor, E7, and E minor 7. All chords are shown at the first fret with the root of F.

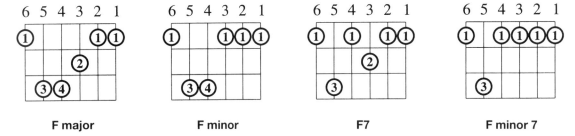

Since bar chords are moveable, all chords are now available to us with just a shift in position. Try the following chord progression that uses bar chords. The number to the right of each chord diagram is the fret at which the chord should be played.

Grunge!

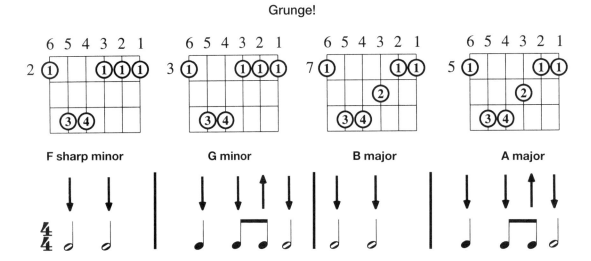

A-form bar chords

The **A-form bar chord** is based around the open position shape of an A chord. This is true of all A-form bar chords. We have moveable chords based on the shape of A, A minor, A 7, A major 7, and A minor 7. All chords are shown at the first fret. A-form bar chords do not use the sixth string. The root for each chord is on the fifth sting.

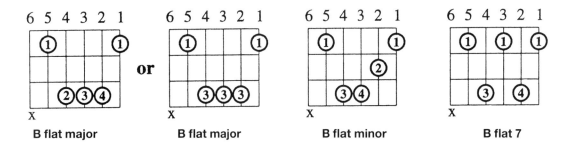

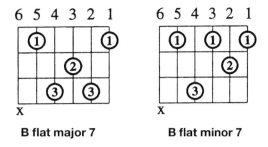

B flat major 7   **B flat minor 7**

Now try the following chord progression using A-form bar chords.

Jazz Time . . .

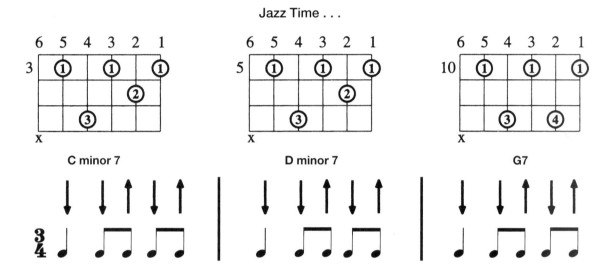

Bar Chords in Classical Music

Bar chords are not limited to popular music. We will find variations of them in all music including many classical works. A bar chord occurs anytime a single finger must hold down more than one string. The following piece is a perfect example.

CD Track 48   Prelude   Matteo Carcassi
(1792–1853)

The chord that occurs in the second measure of the second line is a bar chord. The first finger has to cover both the first and second strings. The symbol above this measure gives us this information.

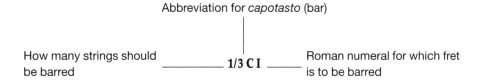

This abbreviation gives us a great deal of information. The C is the abbreviation for **capotasto** the Spanish word for bar. The symbol 1/3 indicates to us that this bar should only cover one third of the strings from high to low. The last symbol I is the Roman numeral one. This indicates the fret where the bar is to be placed.

Chord Break #9 (Rock Pattern)

The following chord progression is similar to many rock progressions of the 70's and 80's. The progression will use bar chords and a new chord: E7 (+♯9).

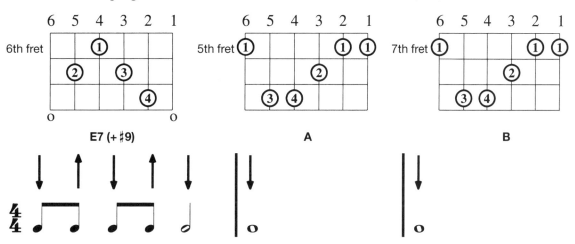

The above progression can be repeated. You may also want to experiment with different rhythms. Following is a solo pattern that uses the **pentatonic minor scale**. You can combine this pattern with the above progression to make a solo.

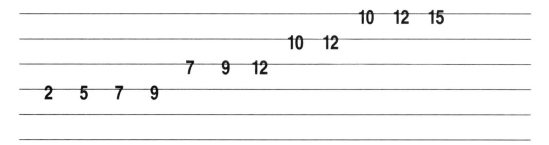

Now that you have the basics down, feel free to improvise using the above pattern.

Harmonics

Harmonics are bell-like sounds that can occur naturally in many places on the guitar. Guitarists use harmonics to tune. We also find harmonics in more advanced pieces.

Although harmonics can be played in almost any position, it is easiest to play them at the fifth, seventh, and twelfth frets. To play a harmonic, lightly touch the string directly above the fret wire. Pluck the string and simultaneously move your left hand finger off the string. The resulting sound is a harmonic.

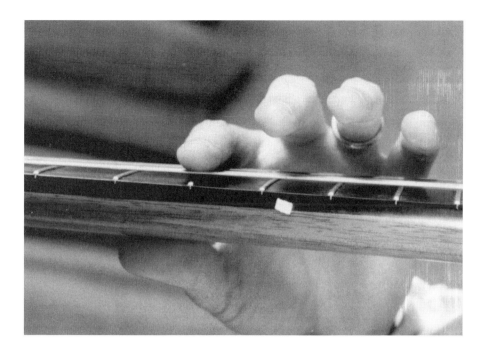

The direction you move away from the string will depend on which string(s) you are playing. If you are playing harmonics on the first, second, or third strings move in a downward direction away from the guitar. If you are playing on any of the lower strings, move upward away from the guitar. This helps to produce a clear harmonic.

Harmonics can be notated in a piece in several ways. The most common is with a diamond-shaped note head indicating the pitch. The string and position of each harmonic are also indicated.

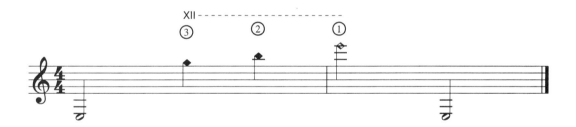

For the above example you would play harmonics at the twelfth fret starting on the indicated strings.

CD Track 49

Harmonic Waltz

PH

Chord Break #10 (Muting)

Frequently guitarists play lines that enhance the rhythm of a song. Since this rhythm guitar part is background to the melody, a technique of slightly damping the sound can be used. This technique is known as **muting**. There are two different muting techniques, one for the left hand and one for the right hand.

Left Hand Muting

The **left hand mute** is easy. To mute with the left hand, slightly release the pressure you are applying to hold down the strings. The result is a percussive sound. Try the following example.

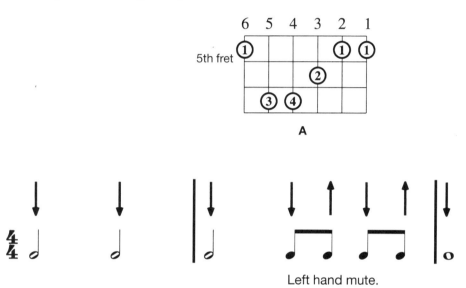

Left hand mute.

Right Hand Muting

Muting with the right hand is almost as easy. To achieve the right hand mute, simply tilt your hand so that your palm is resting on the bridge of the guitar. From this point move slightly forward, toward the neck. When you reach the point just beyond the bridge STOP! Now strum normally but keep your palm in place on the strings/bridge. The resulting muffled sound is a **right hand mute**, which is also known as a **palm mute**. Try the example on the next page.

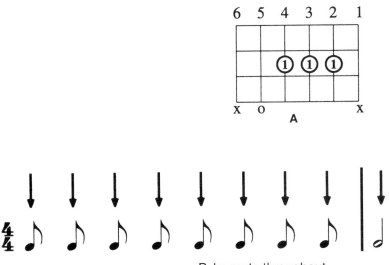

Palm mute throughout.

Now try this example, which uses both left and right hand muting techniques.

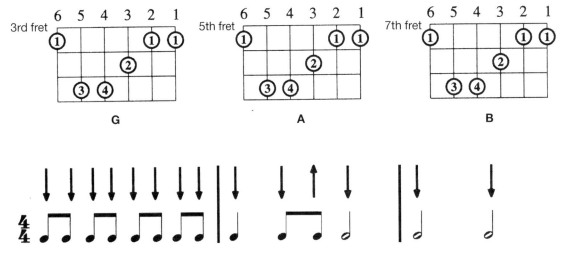

Right hand mute "palm mute."   Left hand mute.

Part III
Technique

The following exercises are designed to help you develop facility and flexibility, which will make more difficult pieces easier to play. I have included an extensive scale section to help you develop speed and accuracy for playing different styles of music.

Many of the exercises that follow will help you to build up strength and endurance in your hands. Work hard but always allow time to relax in between exercises. I suggest spending at least 25 percent of your practice time on technical exercises.

Major Scale (Using 3 Strings)

A **scale** is a series of notes between an octave. Using the first three strings, we can play a major scale. The pattern is as follows:

CD Track 50

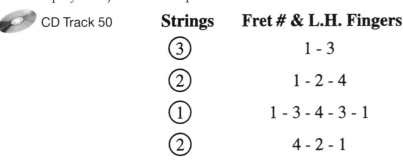

Strings	Fret # & L.H. Fingers
③	1 - 3
②	1 - 2 - 4
①	1 - 3 - 4 - 3 - 1
②	4 - 2 - 1
③	3 - 1

Start the pattern on the third string. Proceed to the first string and then descend back to the third. Try to connect the notes so that no breaks are audible. This scale pattern is moveable. The first note indicates which type of major scale is being played. This note is called the **root**.

You will work on several right hand techniques when practicing this scale. The first is alternating rest strokes. Use the following patterns:

> i m i m . . . etc.
> m i m i . . . etc.
> i a i a . . . etc.
> a i a i . . . etc.
> m a m a . . . etc.
> a m a m . . . etc.
> p i p i . . . etc.
> i p i p . . . etc.

The scale should also be practiced with a pick. Use the following patterns to develop fluid picking technique:

> down stroke—down stroke . . . etc.
> up stroke—up stroke . . . etc.
> down stroke—up stroke . . . etc.

At first practice slowly and emphasize each note. This will help build confidence in these new techniques as well as a clear, defined sound. Speed should not be a factor at first. Over time you will build both the duration and velocity of these exercises.

P-i-m-a Free Stroke Independence

As previously stated, we want our guitar playing to be easy. To help ensure this we must start to achieve independence between our right hand fingers. **Right hand independence** can be defined as the freedom of an individual finger to move or pulse without affecting the other fingers at rest. We have already worked on this concept without knowing it. When you play your musical exercises with alternating i-m rest strokes, you are practicing independent motion between these fingers. We will now start to achieve independence among all of our right hand fingers.

When you play more advanced pieces (which will follow) you will need to use free strokes as well as rest strokes. The following exercises will help you to play even, loud, and independent free strokes. **I suggest using this exercise as a daily warm-up**.

Step 1

Prepare your right hand in this order:

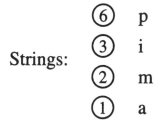

Step 2

Play i but keep your other fingers planted.
Play m but keep your other fingers planted.
Play a but keep your other fingers planted.
Play p but keep your other fingers planted.

Make sure the stroke goes back into your hand. The motion resembles scratching. The key to this exercise is to be sure your other fingers do not move while each individual finger is playing. Practice each individual finger for about thirty seconds.

This exercise also allows us to practice playing loud, clear, free strokes and balance. These techniques will prove useful as we learn more complicated pieces.

The Arpeggio

An **arpeggio** is nothing more than a broken chord. The notes of the chord are played sequentially rather than simultaneously. The study of arpeggios will further our development of right hand finger independence. Use the following right hand position for the following exercises:

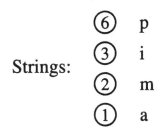

Strings:

Following are all of the possible four-note arpeggio patterns. Let your thumb rest on the sixth string for all of the exercises.

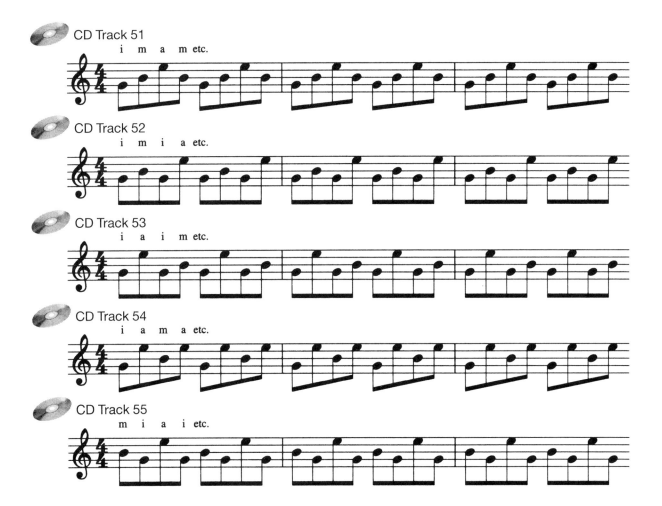

CD Track 56
m   i   m   a etc.

CD Track 57
m   a   m   i etc.

CD Track 58
m   a   i   a etc.

CD Track 59
a   m   i   m etc.

CD Track 60
a   m   a   i etc.

CD Track 61
a   i   a   m etc.

CD Track 62
a   i   m   i etc.

I suggest practicing these patterns daily in conjunction with the previous independence exercise.

The following examples are short arpeggio études (studies).

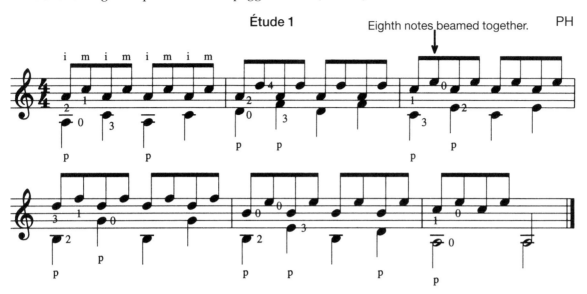

Étude 1 uses an i-m arpeggio with an alternating bass note on every beat. We already know almost all of the chords in this étude. Practice connecting each chord to the next.

Étude 2 uses sixteenth notes ♪. Each sixteenth note is equal to 1/4 beat. This does not mean that you should play the work faster. Just remember that the duration of each beat is dependent upon your tempo.

Use the p-i-m-a arpeggio throughout this étude. Pay special attention to the more difficult chord changes on the second line. Slow practice is the key to success with this piece.

Left Hand Independence Exercises

The following exercises are designed to help you build independence between your left hand fingers. They will also help you refine accuracy when fretting.

Each pattern focuses on the motion between two fingers. I suggest using rest strokes in the right hand and striving for a warm, clear tone.

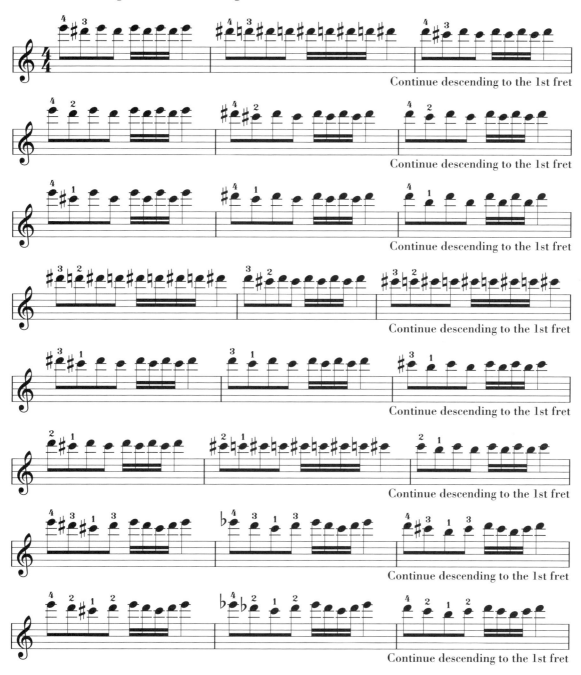

Continue descending to the 1st fret

Continue descending to the 1st fret

Continue descending to the 1st fret

Continue descending to the 1st fret

Continue descending to the 1st fret

Continue descending to the 1st fret

Continue descending to the 1st fret

Continue descending to the 1st fret

More Advanced Scales

The following scale exercises are designed to help you build speed and more advanced technique.

CD Track 64   C Major

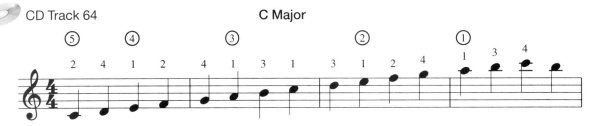

This two-octave scale should be practiced using the following right hand finger combinations. All patterns should be practiced using both free and rest strokes.

i m i m ...etc.
m i m i ...etc.
i a i a ...etc.
a i a i ...etc.
m a m a ...etc.
a m a m ...etc.
p i p i ...etc.
i p i p ...etc.

I also suggest practicing this scale using different rhythms. This changes the accent as well as the rhythmic location of shifts.

CD Track 65   Eighth Notes

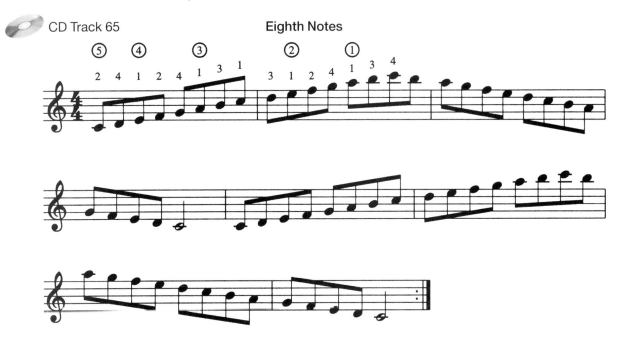

CD Track 66   Triplets

CD Track 67   Sixteenth Notes

This C major scale pattern is moveable. Whatever the starting pitch is becomes the root of the scale.

Daily scale practice is an important element in the refinement of your technique. Although advanced players may practice their scales for hours a day, I recommend less time with more focus for students. Try to allow enough time to push the limits of your technique without limiting your focus to just this topic.

Slow scale practice is very important. You want to play evenly with a loud, clear, full tone. Start out at a slow, comfortable speed. Gradually speed up. Try to practice to the point where your tempo becomes a hindrance. From this point slow down just enough so you are at the edge of your ability. Daily practice in this manner will eventually increase your peak tempo while maintaining your accuracy.

The two most common scales used in popular music for guitar solos are the **pentatonic minor scale** and the **blues scale**. These two scales should be studied in detail with the end goal of speed and accuracy.

The Pentatonic Minor Scale

Unlike the major scale, the **pentatonic minor scale** uses only five different pitches. These pitches are built from the root note. A **root** is defined as the note on which a chord or scale is based.

This is the root position pentatonic minor scale in standard notation. Notice that the scale begins on the note A, which serves as the root. Here is a chart of the same scale:

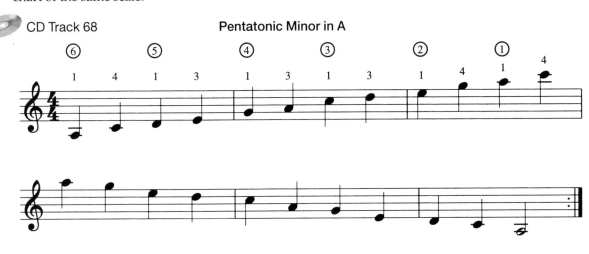

As we can see, there are five different notes in this scale which repeat. We can take these notes and build pentatonic minor scales with the root of A on each of them. Remember: Just because A is not the first note does not mean it is not the root.

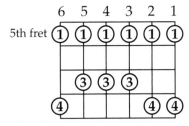

Root Position Pentatonic Minor Scale (A root)
A – C – D – E – G

 CD Track 69

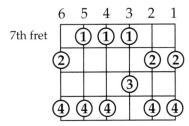

Pentatonic Minor Scale Pattern II (A root)
C – D – E – G – A

 CD Track 70

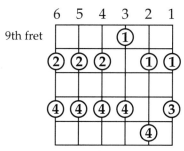

Pentatonic Minor Scale Pattern III (A root)
D – E – G – A – C

 CD Track 71

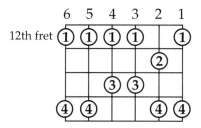

Pentatonic Minor Scale Pattern IV (A root)
E – G – A – C – D

 CD Track 72

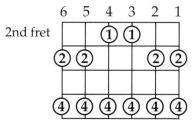

Pentatonic Minor Scale Pattern V (A root)
G – A – C – D – E

These two-octave pentatonic minor scales should be practiced using the following right hand pick patterns:

> down stroke—down stroke . . . etc.
> up stroke—up stroke . . . etc.
> down stroke—up stroke . . . etc.

Your end goal should be even down stroke/up stroke alternation. Practice first at a slow speed, gradually increasing your tempo.

The blues scale looks almost exactly like the root position pentatonic scale. The only difference is the added "blue" note. Notice the extra note on the fifth and third strings. This note gives this scale its distinctive flavor.

This is the root position blues scale in standard notation. Again the scale begins on the note A, which serves as the root. Here is a chart of the same scale:

 CD Track 73   **Blues Scale in A**

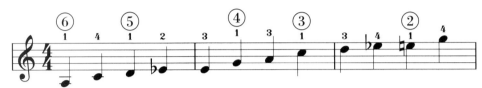

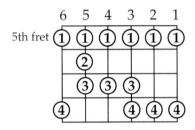

This two-octave blues scale should be practiced using the following right hand pick patterns:

> down stroke—down stroke . . . etc.
> up stroke—up stroke . . . etc.
> down stroke—up stroke . . . etc.

Your goals in practicing this scale should be the same as for the pentatonic minor scale. You now know the two most common scales used in the guitar solos in popular music. Once you become proficient with these patterns, practice improvising within the scale.

All of these scales (pentatonic minor and blues) are moveable.

Example: If you were to begin the root position pentatonic minor scale at the third fret of the sixth string this would be a G pentatonic minor scale in root position.

Following are five modal scales. Each mode has a slightly different flavor to it. Modal scales are used for soloing in a variety of musical styles, including jazz and rock.

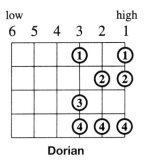

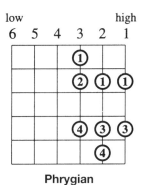

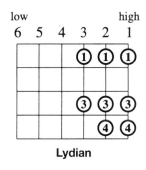

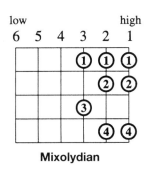

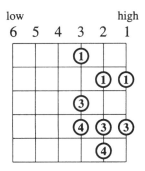

Practice all of these scales using down, up, and alternating down-up right hand picking. These scales are moveable. The first note played is the root of the scale. For example:

Natural minor scale with the root on A (3rd string at the 2nd fret) is an A natural minor scale.

Slurs

Sometimes it is necessary for two or more notes to be as connected as possible. To accomplish this we use **ascending** or **descending** slurs.

Ascending slurs

Ascending slurs are also known as hammer-ons. This is based on the technique used to slur the notes. In the following example a hammer-on is used.

CD Track 74

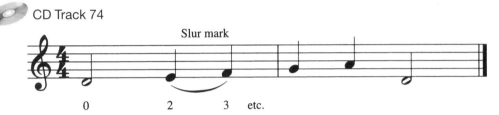

Notice the slur mark connecting the E and F notes in the first measure. To play this ascending slur you should play the E note and hammer your third finger down on the F note. This will change the pitch heard from E to F without any additional right hand articulation. The goal is to produce a hammer-on that sounds similar to a plucked note.

Descending slurs

Descending slurs are also known as **pull-offs**. In the following example a pull-off is used.

CD Track 75

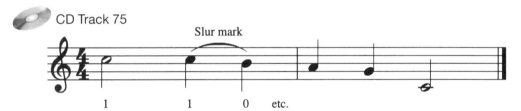

Notice how the slur mark now connects the C and B in the first measure. To play this descending slur you should play the C note and pull your finger off the second string. You should pull-off in a downward direction rather than an outward one. This will produce a change in pitch from C to B without any articulation from the right hand. Again, our goal is to produce two even notes with equal volume without plucking both notes.

As with arpeggios and scales, daily practice is necessary to perfect ascending and descending slurs. The most effective way to achieve this is to focus your practice on specific combinations of individual fingers.

The following ascending and descending patterns should be practiced with specific goals in mind:

1. Try to accent the note being slurred to. This will help to build strength in the slurring finger and thus, independence between each finger.
2. Attempt to match the quality of the sound between the plucked and slurred note.
3. Practice each pattern on every string. The patterns are given on the sixth string but should be repeated on all six strings.
4. Continue each pattern through the seventh fret.

Ascending Slurs (hammer-ons)

Descending Slurs (pull-offs)

Grace Notes

Not all melody notes are created equal. Some notes in a melody are more important than others. One way we can highlight particular notes is with the use of grace notes. Grace notes are single notes or groups of notes that are played on the beat and elaborate a melody note.

    To play the grace note in the second measure simply play the F note and do a quick pull-off to the E note. The F note elaborates the E note.

Now try this piece that includes grace notes.

Study   Mauro Giuliani
                                               (1781–1829)

Part IV
Musical Anthology

CD Track 76   **Andantino in C**   Matteo Carcassi
                                                                                (1792–1853)

This symbol indicates common time (𝄴).

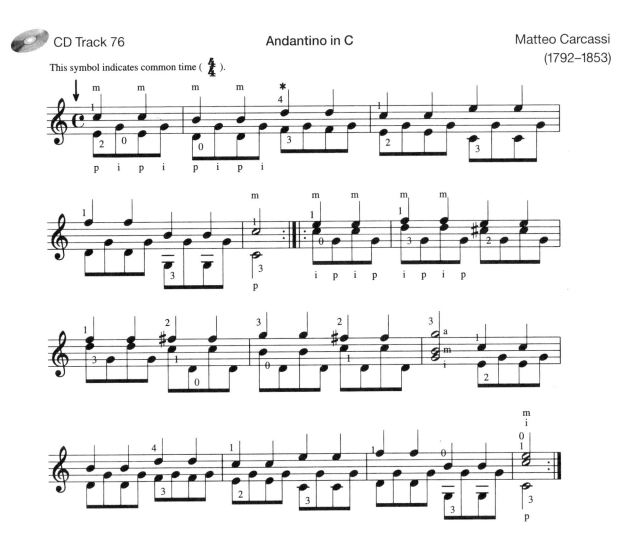

STUDY NOTES FOR ANDANTINO IN C

When learning this piece please pay close attention to the following details:

1. Use the exact fingerings given. Do not substitute other fingerings.
2. At the (*) be sure to use fingers 3 and 4 in the left hand. This will make for an easy change to the next chord.
3. Practice this piece slowly, connecting each chord to the next.
4. Don't forget to repeat each half.
5. Andantino is a slow walking speed.
6. *Have fun!* This is beautiful music.

Matteo Carcassi was a composer and performer with a reputation throughout Europe. He was a contemporary of Ludwig van Beethoven. His compositions range from miniatures to larger concert works.

Two Baroque Dances

CD Track 77 · Mariona · Gaspar Sanz (1640–1710)

CD Track 78 · Danza de las Hachas · Gaspar Sanz (1640–1710)

STUDY NOTES FOR TWO BAROQUE DANCES

Gaspar Sanz composed for a relative of the modern guitar. The 5-course or Baroque guitar was smaller than the modern instrument. Instead of 6 strings, the 5-course guitar had 5 sets of strings. This instrument also utilized a number of different tuning schemes.

Sanz is responsible for one of the most comprehensive guitar tutorials of his time, the *Instrucción de Músic Sobre la Guitarra Española* (1674). "Mariona" and "Danza de las Hachas" are examples of the short dances for the guitar that Sanz is famous for.

The "Mariona" should be played at a lively tempo. The pick-up notes in the first incomplete measure should not be accented. They just help us move rhythmically into the piece. Don't forget to repeat each half.

When practicing the "Danza de las Hachas," try to accent the first beats of each measure. This will accentuate the dance rhythm.

CD Track 79   **Caprice**   Ferdinando Carulli
(1770–1841)

STUDY NOTES FOR CAPRICE

This piece is designed to refine your right hand technique. We are given two lines with different ranges. Be sure to keep the lines independent. Follow all fingerings exactly.

Some other helpful tips include:

1. Be aware of the key signature and the F natural in the second line.

2. Slow practice in the right hand will help resolve tough spots.

3. Isolate tricky sections and practice them away from the piece.

Like Matteo Carcassi, Ferdinando Carulli was known throughout Europe as a composer for the guitar. He lived much of his life in Paris. His compositions range from studies to concerti for guitar.

Prelude in C

Ferdinando Carulli
(1770–1841)

STUDY NOTES FOR PRELUDE IN C

This charming arpeggio piece is a perfect example of Carulli's compositional style in his preludes. The arpeggios outline chords we have already learned. The p-i-m arpeggio should be easily mastered. The practice tempo should be based on the ease of the arpeggio. I suggest a brisk tempo for the final tempo.

As with most arpeggio pieces, the real challenge occurs in the left hand. I suggest you isolate troublesome chord changes and work on them away from the piece. This will make the most efficient use of your practice time.

Allegro

Mauro Giuliani
(1781–1829)

STUDY NOTES FOR ALLEGRO

When studying this piece please pay attention to the following details:

1. Use the exact fingerings given.

2. Be sure to play loud, clear bass notes with your thumb.

3. Don't forget to repeat each half. Also, remember to Da Capo al Fine.

4. *Have fun!*

Mauro Giuliani was one of the most important guitar composers of his time. His compositions for guitar include miniatures, studies, concert works, concerti, and chamber music. He performed throughout Europe. Giuliani also was an accomplished cellist and performed in an orchestra that specialized in the music of Beethoven.

CD Track 80

Andante in G

Fernando Sor
(1778–1839)

STUDY NOTES FOR ANDANTE IN G

This miniature is the perfect study to help us develop the ability to sustain a bass line against a faster-moving melody. Observe all fingerings. Be careful of all accidentals. Remember, they only affect the note they are next to and are negated by the bar line. In addition, watch out for the natural sign (*).

Like Guiliani, Fernando Sor was one of the most influential composers of the 19th century. Sor was born in France but lived much of his life in Spain. His compositions are commonly programmed in recitals. He composed many different types of works for the guitar including miniatures, studies, variation sets (including a very popular one on a theme by Mozart), sonatas, fantasies, and other large solo works.

CD Track 81   **Minuet**   Robert de Visée
                    Transcribed for guitar by Philip Hemmo   (ca. 1660–ca. 1720)

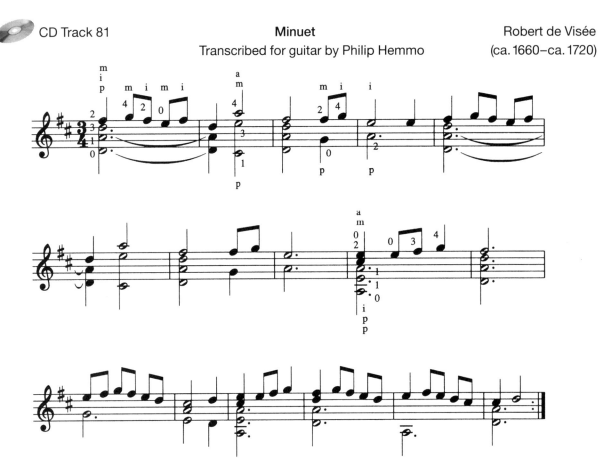

STUDY NOTES FOR MINUET

This short Baroque dance was probably originally composed for the Baroque guitar. The minuet is one of the movements of a Baroque suite. A suite is a set of stylized dances.

The texture of this piece is melody and accompaniment. The accompaniment uses several chords that we know. You should isolate these chord changes and practice them away from the piece. Be sure to hold the chords for their entire duration.

Some other suggestions that will make learning this piece easier include:

1. Observe all fingerings.

2. Remember the key signature.

3. Try to play the first beat of each measure with a slight accent. This will help bring out the dance rhythm of the minuet.

Robert de Visée was a performer and teacher for the French royal court. He published several guitar books, which include many lyrical works like this minuet.

 CD Track 82

Y La Mi Cinta Dorada

Luys de Narváez
(16th Century)

STUDY NOTES FOR Y LA MI CINTA DORADA

This work was originally composed for another relative of the modern guitar, the vihuela. The differences between the vihuela and the modern guitar are few. The vihuela's body shape was a little larger than that of the modern guitar. The overall tuning scheme was quite similar, although a bit higher and with a different tuning for the third string. The vihuela's peak of popularity was from the beginning to the end of the 16th century.

Here are some suggestions that will make learning this piece easier:

1. Observe all fingerings.

2. Remember the key signature.

3. Hold all tied notes for their full duration.

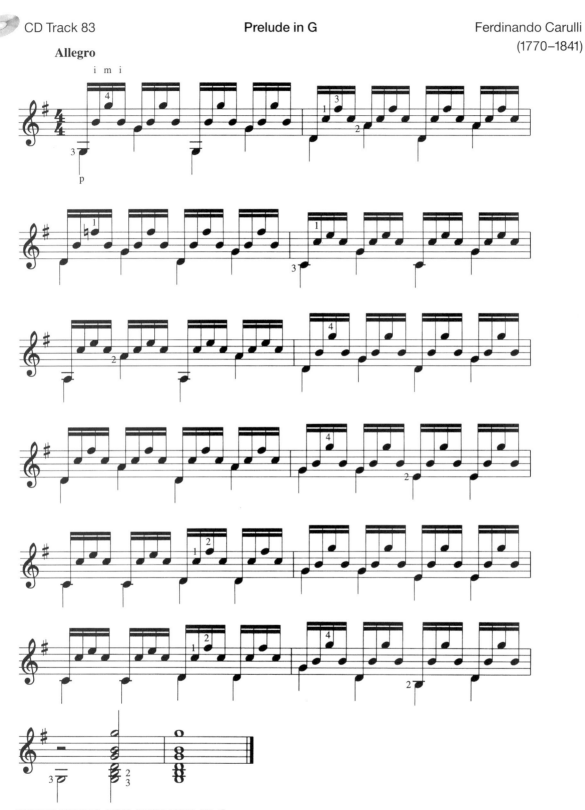

CD Track 83   **Prelude in G**   Ferdinando Carulli
                                                                      (1770–1841)

STUDY NOTES FOR PRELUDE IN G

This arpeggio study uses the p-i-m-i arpeggio exclusively. Remember the key signature has an F sharp. All F notes should be played as F sharp (unless negated by a natural sign ♮). The final two chords should be rolled by strumming with your thumb.

CD Track 84   **Prelude in A**   Ferdinando Carulli
                                                                                      (1770–1841)

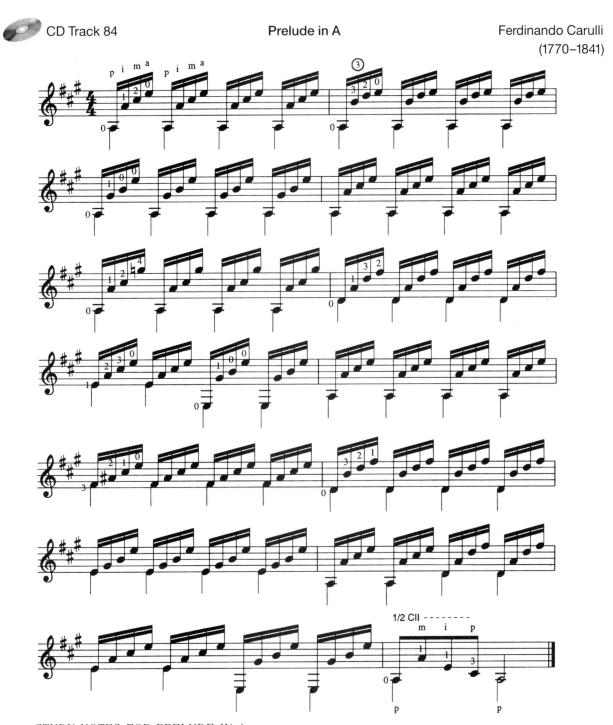

STUDY NOTES FOR PRELUDE IN A

This arpeggio study will help you refine the p-i-m-a arpeggio. As with most arpeggio pieces, the difficulty lies not in the right but in the left hand. To solve this problem, practice thinking about the next chord in the piece rather than the one you are playing. Some other helpful tips include:

1. Use the fingerings that are provided.

2. Isolate troublesome chord changes and practice them away from the piece.

3. Be sure to use a bar for the final chord.

CD Track 85

Andantino in G

Ferdinando Carulli
(1770–1841)

STUDY NOTES FOR ANDANTINO IN G

This charming work helps us refine our technique in several areas including balance and arpeggios. Close examination of this piece shows much repetition of the note G (played on the open third string). When practicing this piece, attempt to de-emphasize this note. It provides a sturdy background but we want to emphasize the melody. Pay close attention to the right hand fingerings given. They will help to eliminate right hand confusion. Be sure to hold the bass notes for their full duration.

Study in A Minor

Mauro Giuliani
(1781–1829)

STUDY NOTES FOR STUDY IN A MINOR

This exciting study focuses on the right hand. The key to mastering this study is the exchange between the thumb and the fingers. Our arpeggio exercises should help prepare you for the task at hand.

Here are some other things to keep in mind when preparing this study:

1. Work out the left hand chord changes. This will help you focus on the right hand.

2. Follow all fingerings exactly.

3. The tempo for this piece should be lively. Work up the tempo gradually.

4. Be aware of the sixteenth note rests.

5. Hold the longer bass notes for their full duration.

6. *Have fun!*

CD Track 86   Andantino   Mauro Giuliani
                                                                      (1781–1829)

STUDY NOTES FOR ANDANTINO

This lyrical work demonstrates how the guitar can imitate the singing voice.
The work opens with a two-part chordal texture much like a vocal duet. Here
are some suggestions to consider when working on "Andantino."

1. Be sure to balance this duet appropriately.
2. Bring out the top melody at the beginning of the second section (*). It is
   repetition of the opening material.
3. Watch this chord change (#); it is tricky!
4. Don't forget to repeat each half.
5. Practice slowly.

Pavana

Transcribed for guitar by Philip Hemmo

Gaspar Sanz

(1674)

STUDY NOTES FOR PAVANA

As with the previous pieces by Gaspar Sanz, "Pavana" is also a type of dance. When practicing this piece try to accent the first beat of each measure. In addition, keep the following in mind when practicing this piece:

1. The intended tempo is slow and stately.

2. Be sure to hold the bass notes for their full duration.

3. Be aware of the accidentals.

4. Practice this section (*) carefully.

Andantino

Fernando Sor
(1778–1839)

STUDY NOTES FOR ANDANTINO

This short work was designed to help us balance a melody against an accompaniment in compound meter. The charming dance rhythm helps push the melody forward. Be sure to count the rhythm out.

Here are several other issues to consider when studying this piece:

1. Slightly accent the first beat of each measure. This will exaggerate the dance rhythm.

2. Practice the slurs away from the piece.

3. Be aware of the rest in the fourth line.

4. Observe all right and left hand fingerings.

CD Track 88   **Andante in C**   Fernando Sor
                                                                        (1778–1839)

STUDY NOTES FOR ANDANTE IN C

This work is another example of Fernando Sor's lyrical compositional style.

1. Pay close attention to right hand fingerings.

2. The section marked (*) uses a middle voice as a pedal (G note).

3. Be aware of the accidentals used in this piece.

4. Don't forget to repeat each half.

5. Practice slowly at first, paying close attention to the rhythm and chord changes.

Ricercar

Transcribed for guitar by Philip Hemmo

Joan Ambrosio Dalza
(1508, Venice)

STUDY NOTES FOR RICERCAR

"Ricercar" was first published in 1508 in a collection entitled *Tablature for Lute.* A lute is a relative of the guitar that was very popular in Italy in the early 1500s. Keep in mind, when studying this piece, that it is intended to be performed at a brisk tempo.

Also, be very careful to use given left and right hand fingerings. They will make it easier to play this piece.

Wilson's Wilde   Anonymous

STUDY NOTES FOR WILSON'S WILDE

This composition was originally composed for lute. The piece uses a simply stated melody, which is then elaborated with eighth notes. The piece has a dance feel to it. I recommend slightly accenting the first beat of each measure. Here are some other study notes to keep in mind when preparing this piece:

1. Follow all fingerings exactly.
2. Remember the key signature.
3. Choose a tempo based on the speed at which you can play the smallest subdivisions.
4. *Have fun!*

CD Track 90

Allegretto Moderato

Fernando Sor
(1778–1839)

STUDY NOTES FOR ALLEGRETTO MODERATO

"Allegretto Moderato" is an advanced piece that will require concentrated study. It is worth it. The end result is a charming two-voiced dance. This piece uses several of the techniques discussed in the technique section, including scales and slurs.

The following suggestions will make the study of this work easier:

1. Be aware of both the time signature and the key signature.

2. Be aware of the accidentals.

3. Remember that there are two lines throughout this piece. Count each line independently.

4. Isolate the measure marked (*). The chord change that occurs is tricky and will need to be practiced away from the piece.

5. Practice slowly.

A Petite Piece

Fernando Sor
(1778–1839)

STUDY NOTES FOR A PETITE PIECE

This two-voice work utilizes many advanced techniques.

1. Be sure to balance each line. You should practice playing each part independently of the other.

2. Watch this chord change (*); it is a little difficult. Extend your fourth finger to get the D♯.

3. Practice this measure (#) slowly while sustaining the low F#.

4. Be sure your slurs are even; don't accent the higher note. Produce a clear pull-off.

5. Utilize slow practice to work out the difficult sections of this piece.

CD Track 91

Adagio

Dionisio Aguado
(1784–1849)

STUDY NOTES FOR ADAGIO

This arpeggio study uses a new subdivision of the beat: the sextuplet. This means each beat is subdivided into six equal parts. The right hand pattern is fairly simple (p-i-m-a-m-i). Isolate this right hand pattern and practice it on open strings until it feels comfortable. The pattern remains consistent throughout the piece.

Also:

1. Be careful of the accidentals. Remember the F# in the key signature.

2. Follow all fingerings exactly.

3. When practicing the section marked with the * be aware of the stretch needed to play the F♯ in the bass. Practice this section slowly until it feels easy.

4. Remember, the overall tempo is slow (adagio). Use this to your advantage.

Op. 6, No. 2

Fernando Sor
(1778–1839)

STUDY NOTES FOR STUDY, OP. 6, NO. 2

This is our most challenging piece so far. This study is designed to work on a specific technical issue: balance. The texture of this work is melody and accompaniment. You must bring out the top line while controlling the dynamics of the lower line. Try to resolve these problems when working on this piece.

1. Connect the top line. It is vocal in nature and should sound continuous.
2. Practice the difficult chord changes slowly so as not to break the continuity.
3. Be careful of the fingerings.
4. Use bars when indicated.
5. Slow practice is essential to play this composition.

CD Track 92

Pavan

Transcribed for guitar by Philip Hemmo

Luis Milán
(1536)

STUDY NOTES FOR PAVAN

Luis Milán lived from approximately 1500 to 1562. Like Narvaez, Milán also composed music for the vihuela. The first publication for the vihuela was Milán's *El Maestro* (1536). This publication contained a variety of works including six stately dances or pavanas. This work is the first of the six. There are many recordings available of these works for you to listen to and study. The set of six pavanas is fairly standard fare on student recitals.

This piece has many challenging elements. Slow practice is essential for the study of this piece. You should also be very conscious of the fingerings that are given. They will save much time in the preparation of this work. The overall tempo should be slow but with motion. Keep these other tips in mind:

1. Try to sustain all tied notes/chords. This helps set up tension against the other moving line.

2. When practicing this section (*) focus on the p-m-i right hand fingering. At first this may seem awkward, but as it becomes more refined you will be able to play quite fast.

3. Practice quick shifts away from the piece. This will help you to work out the trouble spots without playing through the entire work.

Andantino

Fernando Sor
(1778–1839)

STUDY NOTES FOR ANDANTINO

This piece allows us to demonstrate the techniques we have been refining. It presents many advanced concepts. These include melody-accompaniment, use of multivoiced textures, playing in the higher positions, slurs, and bars.

Slow practice will be essential to master this work. You should be aware of the following:

1. Be aware of the key signature and all accidentals.

2. Remember to balance the melody (top line) against the accompaniment.

3. Follow all fingerings exactly.

4. In the section marked with the * count the rhythm out carefully.

5. *Have fun!*

CD Track 93

Étude

Mauro Giuliani
(1781–1829)

STUDY NOTES FOR ÉTUDE

This study is designed to help build independence in the right hand thumb. This is achieved with alternating sections of running eighth notes in the bass and longer bass notes, which harmonically support a faster moving top line. Bring out this contrast. Slow practice is essential to ensure a flowing line. Follow all fingerings exactly. They will make the study of this piece much easier. All dynamics are editorial. However, I feel they enhance the piece.

Works for Guitar Ensemble

The following works for two, three, and four guitars will help refine the skills associated with ensemble playing. When studying these pieces please keep the following concepts in mind:

1. Keep a steady beat throughout each piece. The key to good ensemble playing is the rhythmic unity of all of the players. Practice the more troublesome rhythms away from the piece.

2. At first, work through each piece at a slow tempo. This will help you to identify the more troublesome passages.

3. Observe the key signature and all accidentals.

4. Try to be dynamically balanced. Practice playing so that no one part is louder than the others.

5. *Have fun!*

Red River Valley
Arranged for guitar duo by Philip Hemmo

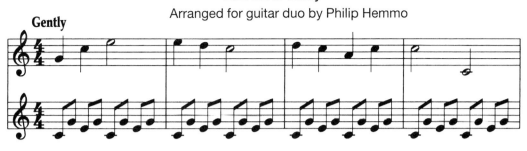

Menuetto and Trio

Transcribed for guitar duo by Philip Hemmo

Wolfgang Amadeus Mozart

(1756–1791)

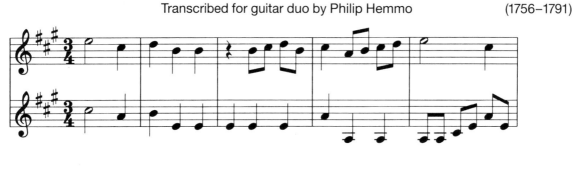

Fine

Trio

Da Capo Menuetto

In the Shade upon the Grass

Christopher Fishburn

Transcribed for guitar duo by Philip Hemmo

Farewell Fair Armida
Transcribed for guitar duo by Philip Hemmo

Robert Smith
(d. 1675)

Fine Knacks for Ladies
Arranged for guitar trio by Philip Hemmo

John Dowland
(1563–1626)

Galliard

Transcribed for guitar trio by Philip Hemmo

Orlando Gibbons
(1583–1625)

Do You Not Know

Transcribed for guitar trio by Philip Hemmo

Thomas Morley
(1558–1603)

Minuet   Johann Sebastian Bach
Transcribed for guitar trio by Philip Hemmo   (1685–1750)

Chorale

Arranged for guitar quartet by Philip Hemmo

Johann Sebastian Bach
(1685–1750)

Trio

Arranged for guitar quartet by Philip Hemmo

Franz Josef Haydn
(1732–1809)

Part V
Appendix

Musical Symbols and Terms

Accidental   A sharp or flat that occurs within a piece of music rather than in the key signature. The sharp/flat applies only to the specific note altered and is negated by the bar line.

Arpeggio   A chord in which the notes are played sequentially rather than simultaneously.

Bar Line   Used in music notation. The vertical line that separates measures.

Chord   Two or more notes played at the same time.

D. C. al Fine   Da Capo al Fine. Instruction to return to the beginning of a piece and proceed until the Fine (end).

Dynamics   Degrees of volume.

Double Bar   Indicates the end of a piece.

Enharmonic   Two notes that sound exactly the same but are written differently (F sharp/G flat).

Free Stroke   A right hand technique where the plucking finger follows through to the back of the hand.

Fret   The space between fret wires.

Flat (♭)   A little (by one fret) lower than the corresponding natural note.

Grace Note(s)   A note or group of notes played on the beat that elaborate a melody note.

Harmonic   A bell-like sound that occurs by touching lightly above the fret wire while plucking.

Hammer-on   An ascending slur.

Key Signature   The placement of sharps and flats at the beginning of each line of music, indicating the key of the piece.

Ledger Lines   The lines above and below the staff that extend the staff.

Measure (Bar)   The space between bar lines.

Notes   Whole Note: (o)
 Half Note: (♩)
 Quarter Note: (♩)
 Eighth Note: (♪)
 Sixteenth Note: (♬)

Octave   Two notes with the same letter name only higher or lower than one another.

Pick–up Notes   An incomplete measure at the beginning of a piece.

Plectrum   A guitar pick.

Pull-off   A descending slur.

Rest   A rhythmic symbol that represents silence.

Rest Stroke   A right hand technique in which the plucking finger follows through to the next string.

Scale   The series of notes between an octave.

Sharp (♯)   A little higher (by one fret) than the corresponding natural note.

Slur   A technique used to connect two or more notes.

Staff   The five lines and four spaces on which music is notated.

Tempo   The speed of the music.

Tie   A curved line ⌣ that rhythmically connects two notes of the same pitch.

Time Signature   A stack of two numbers at the beginning of a piece of music that tells us how many beats per measure and what type of note value equals one beat.

Treble Clef   The clef where guitar music is notated.

Open Position Chords

This page contains a review of all chords used in this book. Use the following page to notate new chords.

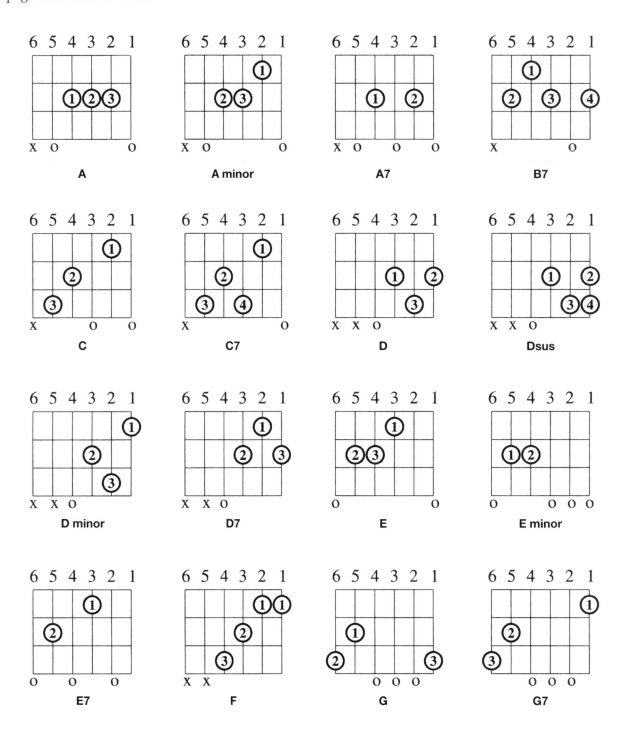

Chord Charts

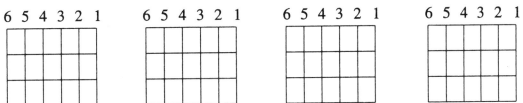

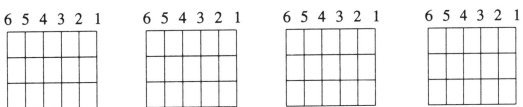

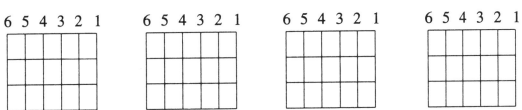

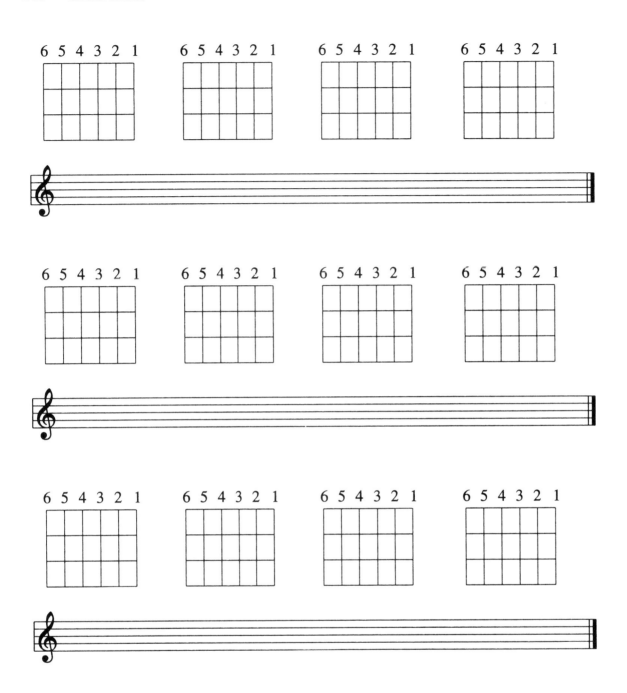

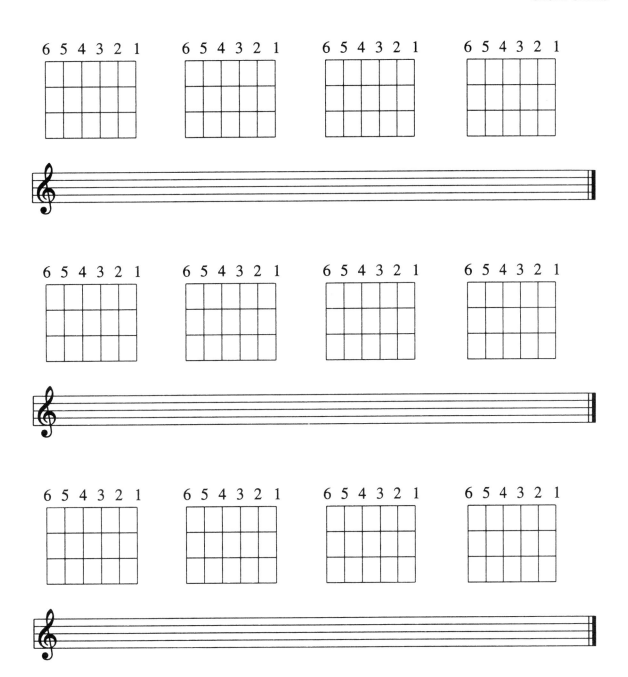